Presented To:

Matthew Stiers

From:

Mom & Earl with Love

Date:

Dec. 25th, 2017

Praise for
Desires of Your Heart and Angels & Cowboys

"Michael has a gift and writes from his heart. He is a true man of God and his words have touched many lives. He sees the beauty in others and shares his life experiences, insights and feelings with honesty and love."- *Nancy from Illinois*

"......his poems have touched my heart.......the poems this gifted man writes are a true inspiration to us all. Michael brings our Heavenly Father's guidance and words of scripture in layman's terms." - *Melody from Texas*

"Your poems saved me Michael; they touched my heart and gave me Peace, the kind that surpasses all understanding. And then you would arm me with the written word and those scriptures became my armor and my shield and soon, I wasn't so sad or discouraged or even ashamed. I'm proud to be a child of God, a horse lover, a cowgirl with those old fashioned morals."- *Maura from Arizona*

"Desires of Your Heart will help you open your heart to hear God speak to you day by day. Your spirit will overflow, as you are embraced by the One who loves you more than you can imagine."- *Debra from Kansas*

"One of the most well written books I have ever read. Each story touches a part of my life in some way. A GREAT spiritual book that I think will even be a BIGGER success than it already is as the public discovers this one. Keep writing Michael Gasaway you have a WINNER on your hands." – *Maddie from Georgia*

"Inspiring, uplifting. Love it !" – *Margaret from Iowa*

"This book is more than just any average book it will speak directly to your heart and the places that need to be filled with encouragement and hope. This book besides my bible itself is so encouraging and full of hope. I truly know it will bless your heart and encourage you!! Truly has a gift for writing from the heart and touches the soul!! Highly recommend this book, it will bless you!! Thank you Michael for your amazing gift of encouragement and writing!!" – *Tiffany from Minnesota*

"You will not be disappointed in his heartfelt writes! A wonderful book! Buy more than one and share to bless others!" – *Cherie from Iowa*

Angels *and* COWBOYS

Stories of Love and Life Written in Rhyme

MICHAEL GASAWAY

© 2015 Michael Gasaway

All rights reserved. No portion of this book may be reproduced, stored in a retrieval system, or transmitted in any form or by any means—electronic, mechanical, photocopy, recording, or any other---except for brief quotation in printed reviews, without prior written permission of the author or publisher.

Published by Diamond G Publishing.

Scriptures were taken from the King James Version of the Holy Bible. Public Domain.

Scriptures were taken from the Holy Bible, New International Version ®, NIV ®. Copyright © 1973, 1978, 1984, 2011, by Biblica, Inc. ™ Used by permission of Zondervan, All rights reserved worldwide. www.zondervan.com The "NIV" and "New International Version" are trademarks registered in the United States Patent Trademark Office by Biblica, Inc. ™ Used by permission

Scriptures taken from the New King James Version®.
Copyright © 1982 by Thomas Nelson, Used by permission.
. All rights reserved.

Scripture quotations are from the ESV® Bible (The Holy Bible, English Standard Version®), copyright © 2001 by Crossway, a publishing ministry of Good News Publishers. Used by permission. All rights reserved.

Cover painting by Denny Karchner. Contact Denny at his web site for more information on this or other western art. **www.karchnerwesternart.com**

Graphic design, front and back cover art by Denny Karchner.

The original cover painting hangs in the Booth Museum of Western Art in Cartersville, GA. **www.boothmuseum.org**

ISBN-13: 978-0692547076

Printed in USA

The stories in rhyme within this book are a work of fiction. Characters, places and incidents either are products of the author's imagination or are used fictitiously. Any resemblance to actual events or locals or persons, living or dead, is entirely coincidence.

This book is dedicated to my family, friends, and anyone that has journeyed down "Life's Highway" in search of your dream. To my sons of whom I'm so proud of the men you have become. To my youngest son Sammy that now inspires us all from heaven above. "Time to go climb that mountain again, Sammy. See you at the top!"

I hope these poems put a smile on your face, a song in your heart or maybe a tear in your eye when you remember back to that first hello or last goodbye. Remember you're never too young or too old to seek out and follow your dreams.
God Bless, Never Give Up and Keep Dreamin'.

Thank you to my many Facebook followers who have taken this journey in rhyme with me. Your comments have been very motivational and kept me writing when I was wondering if it was doing any good.

Follow me on Facebook at: https://www.facebook.com/michaelthepoetryman

Thank you everyone that has offered suggestions for poems. I hope you see a story written in rhyme within these pages that bring you inspiration, faith and peace.

A special thank you goes out to those very exceptional people who inspired many of these poems. May God grant you the desires of your heart and make all your dreams come true.

I would like to extend a very special thank you to Denny Karchner for his time and efforts in producing the graphic art work and cover painting for my books.

Thank you God for guiding my pen that wrote these words. Thank you God for providing me with the inspiration that has touched so many hearts and changed so many lives.

Guide to Story Themes

Adversity: 8, 10, 14, 24, 36, 38, 40, 42, 46, 54, 56, 60, 62, 66, 72, 76, 78, 80, 82, 84, 88, 90, 92, 94, 98, 102, 104, 106, 108, 110, 112, 114, 120, 122, 124, 126, 132, 134, 136, 144, 146, 152

Attitude: 10, 14, 24, 34, 36, 38, 40, 46, 48, 50, 52, 54, 56, 60, 62, 66, 78, 82, 90, 92, 98, 106, 108, 110, 114, 118, 120, 122, 124, 126, 128, 132, 134, 136, 138, 142, 144, 150, 152

Believe: 8, 10, 14, 16, 22, 24, 28, 32, 38, 42, 44, 46, 48, 54, 56, 60, 62, 64, 66, 68, 82, 94, 102, 108, 110, 116, 126, 138, 146, 148, 152

Brokenness: 8, 12, 16, 24, 40, 42, 46, 48, 54, 60, 66, 72, 82, 84, 88, 90, 92, 94, 96, 102, 106, 108, 110, 112, 114, 118, 120, 122, 124, 126, 128, 132, 144, 152

Change: 8, 10, 14, 16, 22, 28, 36, 38, 40, 42, 46, 48, 50, 52, 54, 56, 60, 62, 66, 68, 72, 80, 82, 84, 100, 104, 108, 110, 112, 116, 118, 120, 124, 138, 144, 148, 152

Choices: 8, 10, 12, 14, 18, 22, 28, 30, 32, 34, 36, 38, 40, 48, 50, 52, 54, 56, 60, 62, 66, 72, 78, 80, 82, 84, 88, 90, 96, 98, 100, 102, 106, 108, 110, 112, 118, 120, 122, 126, 128, 134, 136, 138, 144, 146, 150, 152

Closure & Fear: 12, 14, 16, 22, 28, 32, 36, 40, 48, 50, 54, 56, 60, 62, 66, 72, 82, 84, 88, 90, 92, 96, 98, 102, 104, 106, 108, 110, 114, 128, 150, 152

Desires & Dreams: 8, 10, 14, 16, 18, 22, 24, 26, 30, 34, 38, 40, 44, 46, 48, 52, 54, 56, 58, 60, 62, 64, 66, 68, 70, 94, 102, 124, 130, 132, 146, 146, 148, 152

Destiny: 8, 14, 18, 20, 38, 40, 42, 46, 48, 52, 54, 56, 66, 72, 76, 78, 80, 84, 86, 100, 102, 104, 106, 108, 112, 114, 122, 126, 128, 130, 132, 136, 138, 144, 152

Faith: 8, 10, 12, 14, 16, 18, 22, 26, 32, 36, 38, 40, 42, 46, 48, 50, 54, 56, 60, 64, 66, 78, 80, 82, 84, 88, 94, 96, 98, 102, 104, 108, 110, 114, 132, 136, 140, 146, 152

Happiness & Blessings: 8, 10, 14, 16, 20, 22, 24, 26, 28, 30, 34, 38, 40, 44, 46, 52, 56, 58, 60, 64, 68, 70, 78, 102, 114, 116, 130, 140, 148, 152

Hope & Peace: 8, 12, 14, 16, 18, 24, 26, 28, 30, 42, 44, 46, 48, 52, 56, 60, 64, 66, 78, 88, 92, 100, 102, 106, 124, 132, 144, 140, 148, 152

Loss & Pain: 8, 12, 16, 40, 42, 50, 54, 60, 62, 66, 82, 84, 88, 90, 92, 94, 98, 102, 104, 106, 110, 114, 116, 118, 120, 124, 126, 134, 152

Love: 8, 14, 16, 18, 20, 22, 24, 26, 28, 30, 32, 34, 40, 42, 44, 46, 52, 58, 60, 64, 68, 70, 72, 74, 78, 84, 86, 88, 90, 100, 102, 110, 114, 116, 118, 120, 124, 126, 128, 130, 140, 148, 152

New Beginnings: 8, 10, 12, 14, 18, 24, 26, 32, 36, 38, 40, 52, 54, 56, 60, 64, 66, 68, 72, 78, 80, 84, 86, 88, 90, 94, 96, 98, 102, 110, 112, 120, 124, 128, 130, 136, 142, 144, 146, 148, 150, 152

Never Give Up: 8, 10, 14, 18, 20, 26, 28, 32, 36, 38, 40, 42, 44, 46, 48, 52, 54, 56, 60, 62, 64, 66, 76, 78, 80, 82, 84, 88, 92, 94, 98, 100, 102, 106, 108, 110, 112, 120, 124, 126, 128, 130, 132, 136, 138, 142, 144, 146, 148, 150, 152

Passion: 8, 16, 18, 20, 26, 30, 32, 34, 42, 46, 52, 54, 56, 58, 60, 64, 66, 68, 70, 86, 88, 100, 102, 104, 108, 114, 116, 120, 126, 132, 152

Thankfulness: 8, 20, 30, 32, 38, 40, 42, 44, 46, 52, 54, 56, 58, 66, 68, 72, 74, 78, 80, 88, 92, 102, 104, 108, 114, 116, 120, 124, 126, 128, 130, 138, 140, 142, 144, 146, 150, 152

Trust: 16, 20, 24, 28, 32, 36, 42, 44, 46, 48, 52, 54, 56, 58, 60, 64, 66, 80, 88, 94, 98, 102, 110, 112, 120, 124, 128, 136, 138, 140, 144, 146, 150, 152

Table of Contents in Alphabetical Order

62	A Shooting Star
92	A Warrior Once
108	A Warriors Song
8	Angels and Cowboys
124	Because of You
116	Blossom Forth
48	Chasing Her Dreams
132	Complete
94	Cowboy Up!
12	Cowgirl Up!
102	For All Time
130	Forever and a Day
26	Heart to Heart
66	Hopes and Dreams
46	Hope and Peace
72	I Choose You
10	Increase and Blessings
84	Into The Future
138	It's Time
18	Just a Click Away
104	Just a Memory
90	Just Walk Away
54	K'unši
82	Let It Go
64	Life's Dance
110	Lonely Trail
80	Long Live the Cowboy
22	Love's Good Ground
118	Loves Precious Flame
70	Majestic Creatures
32	Moonlit Ride
30	Morphine Lips
58	Mothers Day
56	Mountain Man
74	My Dad
14	New Start
96	No Fear

60	Occupies Her Life and Heart
148	One Day
78	Pay it Forward
144	Perceive, Believe and Receive
150	Reflections
36	Ride Cowgirl Ride
16	Ride Into Your Future
68	River of Love
38	Rodeo and Life
76	Roosevelt's Rough Riders
98	Run to the Roar
44	Shades of Green
136	She Cries Out
34	She Felt a Connection
128	So Right
28	Standing In Front of You
122	Stories and Lies
86	Texas Angel
142	The Cowboy
152	The Cowboy Rides Away
20	The Dance
40	The Moon
50	The Old Ways
112	The Plan
106	The Ranger
140	The Reason
88	The Whiskey
120	Time
24	Valentine's Day Prayer
114	Vaya con Dios, mi Amor
42	Waiting There For Me
52	Westward Bound
100	Wild and Free
134	Words
126	You Never Know
146	You Will Achieve

Michael Gasaway

Angels and Cowboys

Her eyes were so blue they put a Texas sky to shame;
Golden was her hair and glimmered like a dancing flame.

Must be an angel to have survived the life she has seen;
Oh the many tragedies that befell her even before she was a teen.

As a child she was kidnapped at such an early age;
It would have filled anyone else with such an uncontrollable rage.

Neglected by her parents and even abandoned for a time;
No less than an angel could have remained sane in her mind.

An accident that killed her friend and sent her by air flight;
Even this was not enough for her to give up the fight.

Her faith and her trust in God have always remained strong;
Even with all she has faced she vowed to never do another wrong.

A failed marriage and relationships along the way;
But proud she is of her beautiful daughters each and every day.

Yes truly an angel she must be in this world of strife;
She is truly a cowgirl angel trying to find her way through life.

Often she wondered of what her real fate might be;
Then across space and time a cowboy's face she did perceive.

Together they came from different times and places to see;
This cowboy and angel started helping each other to believe.

Now together they ride hand n hand down life's trail ever more;
They have locked away the past behind a closed door.

Yes a special Angel and a Cowboy came together across time;
Now they have been immortalized by words in a rhyme.

So Never Give Up no matter the trials you have faced;
Just keep believing and trusting God and His amazing grace.

~~~

And let us not grow weary of doing good, for in due season we will reap, if we do not give up.
Galatians 6:9

For I know the plans I have for you, declares the Lord, plans for welfare and not for evil, to give you a future and a hope.
Jeremiah 29:11

Love is patient and kind. Love is not jealous or boastful or proud or rude. It does not demand its own way. It is not irritable, and it keeps no record of being wronged. It does not rejoice about injustice but rejoices whenever the truth wins out. Love never gives up, never loses faith, is always hopeful, and endures through every circumstance. Prophecy and speaking in unknown languages and special knowledge will become useless. But love will last forever!
1 Corinthians 13:4-8

Delight yourself in the Lord, and he will give you the desires of your heart. Psalm 37:4

He heals the brokenhearted and binds up their wounds.
Psalm 147:3

For he will command his angels concerning you to guard you in all your ways. Psalm 91:11

Michael Gasaway

Increase and Blessings

She picked up the book from its cover for something to read;
Thinking that maybe within its pages she might find an answer to her need.

Page by page she read stories of her life within;
It told her how she should live her life and how to really win.

How to live a life beyond herself and to really be set free;
Of how to reach out to others in need and overcome adversity.

Increase and blessings she read that God wanted for her in her life;
Just eliminate the negative thoughts and to quit dwelling on her strife.

A Bible verse from her youth came suddenly to her mind;
"As a man thinks in his heart so is he", she realized now was the time.

Time to reprogram her thinking and expect the best with each day yet to come;
To fulfill her dreams and become more than just her average sum.

So now she goes forward expecting God's best each day along her way;
Starting and finishing each day the same, time with God and to pray.

Weeks turned into months as time slowly marched on;
Now she has the future that once she had only dreamt upon.

You have to expect the best in your life for your dreams to come true;
Pray, believe and expect to receive the blessings, God wants to send to you.

Always be thankful to God for guiding your thoughts and steps each day;
Continue to seek His guidance each day as you travel down Life's Highway.

∽∽∽

The L*ORD* *shall increase you more and more, you and your children.*
Psalm 115:14

For as he thinketh in his heart, so is he: Proverbs 23:7

Jabez was more honorable than his brothers; and his mother called his name Jabez, saying, "Because I bore him in pain." Jabez called upon the God of Israel, saying, "Oh that you would bless me and enlarge my border, and that your hand might be with me, and that you would keep me from harm so that it might not bring me pain!" And God granted what he asked.
1 Chronicles 4:9-10

"Give, and it will be given to you. Good measure, pressed down, shaken together, running over, will be put into your lap. For with the measure you use it will be measured back to you."
Luke 6:38

And though your beginning was small, your latter days will be very great. *Job 8:7*

But, as it is written, "What no eye has seen, nor ear heard, nor the heart of man imagined, what God has prepared for those who love him"— *1 Corinthians 2:9*

Michael Gasaway

Cowgirl Up!

The fleeting rays of sunlight danced across the clouds up high;
This was always the time of day those memories rose inside.

"Why", she wondered as that was the question she always asked first;
Not knowing or understanding was like an unquenchable thirst.

She so wanted closure and knowing why was just a part;
This was an open wound she carried deep within her heart.

Sometimes in life we don't know or understand the reason why;
We wonder, we question ourselves through the tears we cry.

Letting go is where you begin and then you start to move on;
Your happiness is not in your past but can be found with tomorrows dawn.

It won't be easy but nothing worthwhile really ever is that;
Don't be a slave to your memories and become an emotional doormat.

The real answers you seek will come to you in due time;
One day you will find closure and peace as another mountain you climb.

So Cowgirl Up, sit tall in the saddle and grab hold of life's reins;
Ride into tomorrow where your heart's dreams you will obtain.

∾∾∾

For God hath not given us the spirit of fear; but of power, and of love, and of a sound mind. 2 Timothy 1:7

"Remember not the former things, nor consider the things of old. Behold, I am doing a new thing; now it springs forth, do you not perceive it? I will make a way in the wilderness and rivers in the desert. Isaiah 43:18-19

And ye shall know the truth, and the truth shall make you free.
John 8:32

Cast all your anxiety on him because he cares for you.
1 Peter 5:7

Blessed are they that mourn: for they shall be comforted.
Matthew 5:4

Trust in the LORD with all thine heart; and lean not unto thine own understanding. In all thy ways acknowledge him, and he shall direct thy paths. Proverbs 3:5-6

And we know that all things work together for good to them that love God, to them who are the called according to his purpose.
Romans 8:28

For I know the plans I have for you," says the LORD. "They are plans for good and not for disaster, to give you a future and a hope. Jeremiah 29:11

Trust in the LORD with all thine heart; and lean not unto thine own understanding. Proverbs 3:5

For everything there is a season, and a time for every matter under heaven: a time to be born, and a time to die; a time to plant, and a time to pluck up what is planted; a time to kill, and a time to heal; a time to break down, and a time to build up; a time to weep, and a time to laugh; a time to mourn, and a time to dance; a time to cast away stones, and a time to gather stones together; a time to embrace, and a time to refrain from embracing; ... Ecclesiastes 3:1-8

Michael Gasaway

New Start

With the beginning of the school year she felt trapped in a job she no longer loved;
Sometimes she all but lost hope and wondered if God had forsaken her from above.

Her love life was similar as she wondered through life with a heart gone lame;
Try as she might each relationship always ended much the same.

Then she heard some advice from a friend that lived so far away;
He spoke words of faith and hope that her dreams could be fulfilled one day.

Saying it was in her hands to do what needed to be done for a bright future to see;
It was up to her to make the necessary changes and then to really believe.

She found it difficult at first but slowly saw the changes happen in her life;
Then one day she awakened with a smile, and gone it seemed was her strife.

Going forward into her new life with that beautiful smile on her face;
Discovering a peace inside she'd never known from God's amazing grace.

Now she has a brand new career fulfilling one of her dreams at last;
It's time for her to completely move forward and let go of her past.

Then one day a cowboy walked in to see her with a purposeful stride;
Little did she know at the time but one day together off they would ride.

Never happier has she been in her life as each new day she does greet;
All it really took was faith in God and leaving her troubles at His feet.

So never give up on your dreams or the desires of your heart;
Trust in God above and let Him lead, guide and direct you to a brand new start.

~~~

Therefore, if anyone is in Christ, he is a new creation. The old has passed away; behold, the new has come. 2 Corinthians 5:17

And I am sure of this, that he who began a good work in you will bring it to completion Philippians 1:6

*Now faith is the substance of things hoped for, the evidence of things not seen.
Hebrews 11:1*

*May the God of hope fill you with all joy and peace in believing, so that by the power of the Holy Spirit you may abound in hope.
Romans 15:13*

For we walk by faith, not by sight: 2 Corinthians 5:7

*I have said these things to you, that in me you may have peace.
John 16:33*

Delight thyself also in the LORD: and he shall give thee the desires of thine heart. Commit thy way unto the LORD; trust also in him; and he shall bring it to pass. Psalm 37:4-5

And let us not grow weary of doing good, for in due season we will reap, if we do not give up. Galatians 6:9

Michael Gasaway

Ride Into Your Future

Sometimes love throws you off and you hit hard;
It can leave you feeling emotionally scarred.

So always climb back on the saddle and get ready to ride;
Life is all about choices you make and you get to decide.

Grab hold of life's reins and put your past and fears behind;
Allow God to let your heart and mind to become aligned.

Ask God to lead, guide and direct this new trail you now follow;
Let Him give you peace inside and you will no longer feel hollow.

Then one day with the rising sun you will see your future bright and clear;
Gone will be all the emotional pain, stress, doubt and fear.

Now ride into your future that God has planned and prepared for you;
Put your trust in Him and to your past memories just bid adieu.

Now riding into her future to follow her dreams and seek her heart's desire;
Finding happiness and peace within is what she did aspire.

She had learned that happiness and peace can't be found by just finding another;
It must be first found within your own heart for you to truly discover.

Then you will find a new love one day when you feel healed and free;
Your new life will then truly begin that you can live it complete and passionately.

~~~

In all your ways acknowledge him, and he will make straight your paths. Proverbs 3:6 ESV

Trust in the Lord with all your heart, and do not lean on your own understanding. In all your ways acknowledge him, and he will make straight your paths. Proverbs 3:5-6 ESV

And the Lord will guide you continually and satisfy your desire in scorched places and make your bones strong; and you shall be like a watered garden, like a spring of water, whose waters do not fail. Isaiah 58:11 ESV

*For God gave us a spirit not of fear but of power and love and self-control.
2 Timothy 1:7 ESV*

Now may the Lord of peace himself give you peace at all times in every way. The Lord be with you all. 2 Thessalonians 3:16 ESV

Delight yourself in the Lord, and he will give you the desires of your heart. Psalm 37:4

He heals the brokenhearted and binds up their wounds. Psalm 147:3

And we know that all things work together for good to them that love God, to them who are the called according to his purpose. Romans 8:28

Michael Gasaway

Just a Click Away

She was growing weary and thought about giving up;
Was it really possible on the internet to find your true love?

This was all so new and how strange it all seemed;
Only her best friend knew about this internet dating scheme.

Then came that fateful day, and there he stood on her screen in that Stetson hat;
Pondering she thought, "Should I reply and answer his kind words back?"

Then in an instant she thought why not reply back to him;
After all he really looks so good in those wranglers with that cowboy grin.

So back and forth they typed for hours it seemed;
Many times she wondered if this was just some romantic dream.

They went from typing to talking as their feelings seem to grow;
But once she heard his voice, something inside of her said, 'don't let this one go'.

Days turned to weeks and they knew they must meet what else could they do?
Each needed to know if what they were feeling was really true.

The date was set and off to him she would fly;
Yes she thought, 'just one more time I'll give true love another try'.

There he stood as she walked from the plane;
Something inside of her said, 'you'll never be the same'.

Their eyes met and into his arms she came;
They kissed softly at first then passionately as loves embers turned into a flame.

That flame grew and still burns to this day, as the years have gone by;
Yes they found true love on the internet and together now they still ride, side by side.

You never know how your true love story may unwind;

So just pray to God and believe that your true love someday you will find.

Don't give up; just have faith that your true love will come one day;
Your destiny and true love could be just a click away.

So lift up a prayer for the lonely hearts everywhere tonight;
That their prayers are answered and true love they may find, even if on an internet dating site.

This is a poem about a true love written in words and rhyme;
Yes, a real true love story of some friends of mine.

~~~

Beloved, let us love one another, for love is from God, and whoever loves has been born of God and knows God.
1 John 4:7

Let all that you do be done in love. 1 Corinthians 16:14

And above all these put on love, which binds everything together in perfect harmony. Colossians 3:14

And above all these put on love, which binds everything together in perfect harmony. Colossians 3:14

Delight yourself in the Lord, and he will give you the desires of your heart. Psalm 37:4

Michael Gasaway

The Dance

He placed his arms around her as she cooked at the stove;
Twirling her around and taking her out onto the patio through the alcove.

The rain was just starting to gently fall from the sky above;
Taking her into his arms they danced a dance of pure love.

Holding each other closer as they continued on with their dance;
Drops of rain seemed to just intensify the air with romance.

Tears mingled with the drops of rain as they rolled down her face;
Inside her heart she was feeling an amazing amount of grace.

As the rain continued to softly fall, on they danced holding each other tight;
It was an emotional and spontaneous dance of love on that night.

Coming inside later and each helping the other get dry;
She could no longer hold the tears back and started to cry.

He gently kissed the tears from her cheeks as they fell;
Inside her heart she could feel her love for him start to swell.

Looking deep into her brown eyes, he kissed her passionately once more;
"I just wanted you to know of my love for you, the one I truly adore."

Time has gone on and that is still one of their fondest memories of all;
Memories always come flooding back anytime that the rain starts to fall.

True love is normally made of little things that we do for one another;
How we try to please the other and in doing so, a deeper love we discover.

Next time you're with the one that you do love and adore;
Pray for rain and then closely dance together, all the way out the door.

Enjoy the simple things in life together, like rain and the stars in the sky;
Always hold hands and show your love for each other and it will intensify.

Never give up on love or each other and never let loves fires dwindle;
The reason God brought you together was not accidental.

∼∼∼

Let all that you do be done in love. 1 Corinthians 16:14

And above all these put on love, which binds everything together in perfect harmony. Colossians 3:14

*Beloved, let us love one another, for love is from God, and whoever loves has been born of God and knows God.
1 John 4:7*

A time to weep, and a time to laugh; a time to mourn, and a time to dance; Ecclesiastes 3:4

Praise him with tambourine and dance; praise him with strings and pipe! Psalm 150:4

Michael Gasaway

Love's Good Ground

The sun will rise and the sun will set;
And each day we must strive to do our best.

Every day is a gift from God up above;
That He sends to us with His perfect love.

How we live this day He leaves up to you and me;
It's up to us to live it completely and regret free.

Go put a smile on your face as the new day does begin;
Let go of your fears, setting them free into the wind.

Look forward to this new life that you have found;
Plant your seeds of love and trust in this good ground.

Never worry about what tomorrow may bring;
Just look toward heaven and to Him do praise and sing.

In this good ground, the seeds of love you plant this day;
Will always blossom and unconditional love will come to stay.

Nurture this new love and each other as long as you both shall live;
Place a hedge of protection and faith all around, is imperative.

Protect it from the weeds of adversity and together pray over it each night;
Love one another as God does, unconditionally, unselfishly with all your might.

Spiritually water your love always with care and watch it grow;
So that together you will always be, as you both grow old.

This is a love story of unconditional love and how it should be;
About how love should be nurtured so that God's blessings, you will always see.

~~~

But he that received seed into the good ground is he that heareth the word, and understandeth it; which also beareth fruit, and bringeth forth, some an hundredfold, some sixty, some thirty. Matthew 13:23

But that on the good ground are they, which in an honest and good heart, having heard the word, keep it, and bring forth fruit with patience. Luke 8:15

Do not be anxious about anything, but in everything by prayer and supplication with thanksgiving let your requests be made known to God. And the peace of God, which surpasses all understanding, will guard your hearts and your minds in Christ Jesus. Philippians 4:6-7

Let all that you do be done in love. 1 Corinthians 16:14

Love is patient and kind; love does not envy or boast; 1 Corinthians 13:4

And above all these put on love, which binds everything together in perfect harmony. Colossians 3:14

Delight yourself in the Lord, and he will give you the desires of your heart. Psalm 37:4

Michael Gasaway

Valentine's Day Prayer

A delicate rose was she among the thorns of life;
In her time she had seen more than her fair share of sadness and strife.

Life hadn't made her bitter, but only better it seems;
Nightly she still prayed for the answer to her heart's dreams.

Her dream was to have that one special man to love;
How she hoped that this year, her prayer would be answered from above.

Then one star filled Texas night he came strolling by;
At that special moment, he smiled and instantly, caught her eye.

They held each other close with their eyes, as her heart began to race;
In her mind she wondered if this was the beginning of love's special embrace.

With a tip of his hat and a smile on his lips;
She prayed this would be more than just another failed relationship.

Hello Darlin' were the first words she heard him say;
His deep voice made her feel like she was part of some romantic play.

Oh how she had prayed each night for that special "one";
But each time, she'd been left, with her heart once again broken.

Was he the one, the answer to her many prayers each night;
Then he asked her to dance, her heart jumping with delight.

Dancing and talking the time went by way too fast;
Each wondered secretly if this was something that was destined to last.

Now together under the stars, they walk, hand n' hand;
For now at least, they are no longer a part of loves wasteland.

Their story has only just begun; neither knows what the future may hold;
But together into tomorrow, they both boldly go.

So lift up a prayer for star struck lovers everywhere this Valentine's Day;
That each will find true love along "Life's Highway".

~~~

Anyone who does not love does not know God, because God is love. 1 John 4:8

And above all these put on love, which binds everything together in perfect harmony. Colossians 3:14

But the fruit of the Spirit is love, joy, peace, patience, kindness, goodness, faithfulness, Galatians 5:22

Let all that you do be done in love. 1 Corinthians 16:14

*Beloved, let us love one another, for love is from God, and whoever loves has been born of God and knows God.
1 John 4:7*

*Love is patient and kind. Love is not jealous or boastful or proud or rude. It does not demand its own way. It is not irritable, and it keeps no record of being wronged. It does not rejoice about injustice but rejoices whenever the truth wins out. Love never gives up, never loses faith, is always hopeful, and endures through every circumstance. Prophecy and speaking in unknown language and special knowledge will become useless. But love will last forever!
1 Corinthians 13:4-8*

We love because he first loved us. 1 John 4:19

Michael Gasaway

Heart to Heart

Her eyes are a blue as the sky in a Texas spring;
How her golden hair shines like that of an angels wing.

Having known both happiness and sadness in her life;
Trusting in God has taught her that He will deliver her from all strife.

Heart to Heart is how she knows it will be one day soon;
She sees a special cowboy and her riding beneath a Texas moon.

Hearts just seem to abound everywhere she looks;
On a pony's coat, a rock, clouds in the sky or within a book.

Each day a new heart she does find as she goes about;
In her mind its God's way of showing her to never doubt.

Then one day he came strolling by and caught her eye;
Was he the one she thought, to ride with her through life, side by side.

The days, weeks and months just seemed to go by in a daze;
That's how it sometimes goes, when you enter into love's haze.

Now together they ride hand n hand into the setting sun;
Two special hearts were brought together and now beat as one.

Never give up on your dreams or the desires of your heart;
Ride into tomorrow trusting in God as He leads you into a fresh new start.

For God knows the perfect time and place of all the things we need;
Just keep believing and one day your dream you will receive.

~~~

"And whatever you ask in prayer, you will receive, if you have faith." Matthew 21:22

And without faith it is impossible to please God, because anyone who comes to him must believe that he exists and that he rewards those who earnestly seek him. Hebrews 11:6

Now faith is the substance of things hoped for, the evidence of things not seen. Hebrews 11:1

For still the vision awaits its appointed time; it hastens to the end— it will not lie. If it seems slow, wait for it; it will surely come; it will not delay. Habakkuk 2:3

Wait on the LORD: be of good courage, and he shall strengthen thine heart: wait, I say, on the LORD. Psalm 27:14

Because to every purpose there is time and judgment, therefore the misery of man is great upon him. Ecclesiastes 8:6

To everything there is a season, and a time to every purpose under the heaven: Ecclesiastes 3:1

Delight thyself also in the LORD: and he shall give thee the desires of thine heart. Psalm 37:4

And let us not grow weary of doing good, for in due season we will reap, if we do not give up. Galatians 6:9

Michael Gasaway

Standing In Front of You

Her dark hair brushed across her face in the gentle mountain breeze;
Change was in the air as the leaves began to turn high in the trees.

Thinking back on the past year and the changes she had seen;
The sunlight danced in her azure blue eyes as she looked upon this beautiful scene.

This was the time of year for change and reflections of the past;
Knowing this was the time to move forward and to be free at last.

Free from her memories and those that had done her wrong in life;
Really putting away the past this time along with all of life's strife.

Dealing with all these difficulties, she had discovered God's love from above;
Her life she knew was now in His hands and she began trusting in God's unconditional love.

Now she was ready to move forward and truly let God guide her way;
She knew that she must continue trusting God and this time from His word never to stray.

Little did she know or could she really in her mind completely understand;
God was just waiting on her to change before sending that one special cowboy man.

God can lead, guide and direct us in life, but it is up to us to really follow;
If we continue to go off course and go our own way, then we will continue to feel hollow.

So go into the future and really believe in your dreams with your head held high;
Trust in God for the best in life and never settle to just get by.

Thank God each day for this life and believing your dreams will still come true;
One day the desires of your heart, you will realize are standing right in front of you.

For everything there is a season, and a time for every matter under heaven:
Ecclesiastes 3:1

Do not be anxious about anything, but in everything by prayer and supplication with thanksgiving let your requests be made known to God. And the peace of God, which surpasses all understanding.
Philippians 4:6-7

Behold, I am doing a new thing; now it springs forth, do you not perceive it? Isaiah 43:19

Then the Lord God said, "It is not good that the man should be alone; I will make him a helper fit for him." Genesis 2:18

Delight thyself also in the LORD: and he shall give thee the desires of thine heart. Commit thy way unto the LORD; trust also in him; and he shall bring it to pass. Psalm 37:4-5

The Lord is my strength and my shield; in him my heart trusts, and I am helped; my heart exults, and with my song I give thanks to him. Psalm 28:7

Michael Gasaway

Morphine Lips

It was for them merely just a first date;
Neither one even considered that it might be fate.

He met her at the door with a tip of his hat and a Hello Darlin';
She didn't understand what this was that she was feeling.

Taking her arm he escorted her inside to her chair;
He is not what she expected now caught completely unaware.

She had it all planned in her mind from the very start you see;
Just to meet and at the most maybe a friend he might just be.

Of many things they talked and discussed through the night;
She hung on his every word; it was all feeling oh so right.

His touch on her arm was like nothing she had ever felt before;
It was like electricity reaching down to her very core.

She couldn't remember smiling so much or feeling so alive;
Dormant feelings were being awakened deep inside.

Closer she sat to him as they talked on through the evening hours;
She kept thinking after this I'm going to need a cold shower.

The evening drew to a close much too quickly for them;
But as with all good things they eventually come to an end.

He walked her out the door with his arm around her waist;
All at once she was spinning around and she felt his hands gently caress her face.

Their lips touched gently at first;
Then passion over took them and WOW she thought what a kiss.

This was a kiss like she had never felt in her life before;
She knew in an instant that she wanted a whole lot more.

So alive, happy and special she felt, he had touched her deep within;
It made her feel alive when his fingers touched her skin.

Morphine lips are what she kept pondering to herself inside;
His kisses are really beginning to make me feel high.

What a kiss is all she kept thinking as hand n' hand they walked on through the night;
Was this a dream and is he for real, it all seems oh so right.

∼∼∼

Let him kiss me with the kisses of his mouth! For your love is better than wine;
Song of Solomon 1:2

Let love be genuine. Abhor what is evil; hold fast to what is good.
Romans 12:9

With all humility and gentleness, with patience, bearing with one another in love,
Ephesians 4:2

Love bears all things, believes all things, hopes all things, endures all things.
1 Corinthians 13:7

So now faith, hope, and love abide, these three; but the greatest of these is love.
1 Corinthians 13:13

Michael Gasaway

Moonlit Ride

Looking to the horizon she saw the sun start to sink into the west;
Turning she saw to the east the full moon rising to begin its nightly quest.

Soon a blanket of stars would fill the Texas sky above;
Oh how she dreamed of sharing this with her one true love.

It had been so many years since she had let a man get near;
Shattered dreams and a broken heart had left her with just her fear.

Fear of the unknown and of the pain she had known in her past;
Maybe it was time she thought to give it one more try and this time it would last.

Should she let him into her life and take another chance on love;
This is what she had been praying for each night to God above.

He seemed so different than any other man that had crossed through her life;
This cowboy had an inner strength with eyes that also had seen their share of strife.

Why not she thought as she was so tired of being alone with just her dog and horse;
He could be the one sent from above to ride with her and set a new course.

You can't win if you never take a chance and give it another try;
Then as if on cue the stars began to dance in her dazzling violet eyes.

She pictures this cowboy and her taking their first moonlit ride;
There they go in her mind with the moon glimmering off her raven hair side by side.

Now together they ride hand n hand beneath a full moon shining so bright;
They had both taken another chance on love and it was for both feeling so right.

Sometimes Gods perfect timing is all that you really need;
Just step out on faith, keep praying and let God have the lead.

∽∽∽

For God hath not given us the spirit of fear; but of power, and of love, and of a sound mind.
2 Timothy 1:7

For I know the plans I have for you, declares the Lord, plans for welfare and not for evil, to give you a future and a hope.
Jeremiah 29:11

See, I am doing a new thing! Now it springs up; do you not perceive it?I am making a way in the wilderness
and streams in the wasteland.
Isaiah 43:19

There is no fear in love, but perfect love casts out fear. For fear has to do with punishment, and whoever fears has not been perfected in love.
1 John 4:18

Yet you do not know what tomorrow will bring. What is your life? For you are a mist that appears for a little time and then vanishes.
James 4:14

Michael Gasaway

She Felt a Connection

Oh how her blonde hair glistens in the Colorado sun;
Her brown eyes look into his and she remembers back to when they became one.

It was almost at first glance upon seeing him she just knew;
Inside she felt a connection as her feelings over time grew.

He was her protector and trusted friend along many a trail;
On him she knew that she could always depend and that her, he would never fail.

Most people won't understand this story that I write;
For it's not about a man at all, but a horse whose coat was pure white.

They had bonded together her and this horse named Slick;
Didn't take long as closer they became; it seemed to happen so quick.

Many years ago he had come into her life to stay;
The scores of trails they had ridden by both night and day.

Some may call it an obsession but I call it passion and love;
It's a special bond between this woman and her horse that came from God above.

Not everyone can find that one truly special horse in their life;
She had been blessed to have found him at a time that helped her deal with her strife.

How she smiled remembering, riding him with the wind upon her face;
Riding across the plains just her and Slick and feeling God's amazing grace.

It takes a special woman to connect with a horse in this way;
Their minds became one but no words did she ever have to say.

A soft touch and gentle pressure from her knees was how she spoke as she rode;
This was a special gift between them that from above had been bestowed.

Yes horses are special; this she feels deep within her heart;
And with them she knows she will always want to be a part.

Horses are exceptional creatures and what she truly loves the best;
For unlike people, a horse will always pass her test.

~~~

And whatsoever ye do, do it heartily, as to the Lord, and not unto men; Colossians 3:23

I will instruct you and teach you in the way you should go; I will counsel you with my eye upon you.
Psalm 32:8

Fulfill ye my joy, that ye be likeminded, having the same love, being of one accord, of one mind. Philippians 2:2

Do everything in love. 1 Corinthians 16:14

Michael Gasaway

Ride Cowgirl Ride

Sometimes love throws you off and you hit hard;
It can leave you feeling emotionally scarred.

You can just lie there and feel sorry for yourself and give in;
Or pick yourself up, dust yourself off and begin again.

Climb back on the saddle and forget the tears you cried;
Life is about choices you make and you get to decide.

Ask God to lead, guide and direct this new trail you travel down;
He will show you the way and peace within will abound.

Then one day with the rising sun, you will see your future bright and clear;
Gone will be all the emotional pain, doubt and fear.

So now ride into your future that God has planned for you;
Put your trust in Him and to your past just bid adieu.

You won't know what lies over that next mountain until you try;
So Cowgirl Up and Ride Cowgirl Ride.

~~~

Trust in the LORD with all thine heart; and lean not unto thine own understanding. In all thy ways acknowledge him, and he shall direct thy paths. Proverbs 3:5-6

And the Lord will guide you continually and satisfy your desire in scorched places and make your bones strong; and you shall be like a watered garden, like a spring of water, whose waters do not fail. Isaiah 58:11

For God hath not given us the spirit of fear; but of power, and of love, and of a sound mind. 2 Timothy 1:7

Now the Lord of peace himself give you peace always by all means. The Lord be with you all. 2 Thessalonians 3:16

Delight yourself in the Lord, and he will give you the desires of your heart. Psalm 37:4

The heart of man plans his way, but the Lord establishes his steps. Proverbs 16:9

Michael Gasaway

Rodeo and Life

Life is no different than a rodeo if you ponder on it for awhile;
You pay your money and take your chances and try to do it with style.

It's not about whether or not you'll get thrown to the ground in life;
Like the rodeo you will, it's just a matter of time and during what strife.

The question is will you get back on the saddle of life and ride again;
Or will you just sit in the dust of despair and give in?

Are you going to grab hold of life's reins and give it another try?
This time hanging on and making it through an eight second ride.

Maybe you're chasing life like the barrels you run for time;
You're going so fast in life that it's just a blur as you cross the line.

Each time you ride a new life lesson on life you get to learn;
Then one day as the buzzer sounds and the gold buckle you finally earn.

Forget all the tough times and trials you have faced along the way;
Just sit tall in the saddle and know that God is riding with you each day.

Now go out each day and ride through life giving it all you've got to give;
This is your time and your chance is now, to once again start to live.

Yes, life is a lot like a rodeo and each brings new challenges to face;
Always do what's right and God will lead you with His amazing grace.

~~~

*Hatred stirs up conflict, but love covers over all wrongs.
Proverbs 10:12*

*I can do all things through Christ which strengthened me.
Philippians 4:13*

And let us not grow weary of doing good, for in due season we will reap, if we do not give up. Galatians 6:9

*For with God nothing shall be impossible.
Luke 1:37*

*For I know the plans I have for you, declares the Lord, plans for welfare and not for evil, to give you a future and a hope.
Jeremiah 29:11*

But you, take courage! "Do not let your hands be weak, for your work shall be rewarded." 2 Chronicles 15:7

*And we know that all things work together for good to them that love God, to them who are the called according to his purpose.
Romans 8:28*

Rejoice always, pray without ceasing, give thanks in all circumstances; for this is the will of God in Christ Jesus for you. 1 Thessalonians 5:16-18

Michael Gasaway

The Moon

Sometimes she stops and looks up at the moon and thinks of him;
She wonders if somewhere he's looking up at it too, remembering his grin.

Days and weeks slowly passed by and turned into years;
Nothing left inside as she has already cried all the tears.

Late at night sometimes before she drifts off to sleep her thoughts turn to him in review;
It's that quiet time of night just before the stars turn blue.

Inside her heart she knows a part of her will always be empty inside;
That is the part of her heart she left inside of him and will always reside.

The scars are covering the pain and hurt she suffered down deep;
On now she travels alone with just her memories to keep.

Someday God may smile on her once again and lead her to love;
But she knows now that it's all up to Him high above.

So each night she prays that he's safe and finds love and happiness once again in his life;
And that the fear will leave him along with all of life's strife.

God bless all the broken hearts out there far and wide;
Only God, time and tears will heal what is broken deep inside.

As the healing goes on day after day with God's help from above;
Just know that He is always with you showing you His unconditional love.

Then one night under the moon and a sky full of stars;
Into her life walked that special cowboy to the sound of distant guitars.

This is her new life about to begin for never giving up and trusting in Him;
Now hand n' hand she walks under that blue moon ready to start living again.

∾∾∾

The Lord is near to the brokenhearted and saves the crushed in spirit. Psalm 34:18

Casting all your care upon him; for he careth for you. 1 Peter 5:7

They that sow in tears shall reap in joy. Psalm 126:5

For with God nothing shall be impossible. Luke 1:37

And let us not grow weary of doing good, for in due season we will reap, if we do not give up. Galatians 6:9

For I know the thoughts that I think toward you, saith the LORD, thoughts of peace, and not of evil, to give you an expected end. Jeremiah 29:11

"He will wipe away every tear from their eyes, and death shall be no more, neither shall there be mourning, nor crying, nor pain anymore, for the former things have passed away." Revelation 21:4

Michael Gasaway

Waiting There For Me

Life is not about the things in life you can do without;
It's about learning to live life without the things you most care about.

Life is ever changing as the years go by;
We never know what we can do until one day we really have to try.

Sometimes just when you think you have won life's race;
Your knocked down and thrown flat on your face.

Thinking that your life is so grand you have all that you ever dreamed;
Then one day it all comes apart at the seams.

One day the love of your life is stricken and taken away;
Leaving you wondering how to live without them and go on another day.

But go on you must, even when you feel like dying;
You can't give up now and just stop trying.

Just when you think you've seen the worst that life has to offer this day;
Another challenge is placed in your way.

I don't understand why some people are tested with such trouble;
Then later God will restore it all, even more than double.

Some things in life cannot be replaced for me;
Like her smiling face and holding her hand on a summers eve.

Sometimes God will restore here and now what was taken away;
Or makes you wait until you get to heaven so you can spend forever and a day.

That is how I know that to heaven I must go for her to see;
As in heaven she will be waiting there for me.

Believing God brought us together as we were always meant to be;
Together in heaven is where we will spend eternity.

Without her I may have to live for a time down here;
Someday I'll get to hear her charming angel voice again sweetly in my ear.

So I must be good and the Bible I must read and heed;
Because My Darlin' is in heaven, waiting there for me.

~~~

Love bears all things, believes all things, hopes all things, and endures all things. 1 Corinthians 13:7

*Return to your fortress, you prisoners of hope; now I announce that I will restore twice as much to you.
Zechariah 9:12*

O death, where is thy sting? O grave, where is thy victory? The sting of death is sin; and the strength of sin is the law. But thanks be to God, which giveth us the victory through our Lord Jesus Christ. 1 Corinthians 15:55-57

*He will wipe away every tear from their eyes, and death shall be no more, neither shall there be mourning, nor crying, nor pain anymore, for the former things have passed away."
Revelation 21:4*

*In my Father's house are many mansions: if it were not so, I would have told you. I go to prepare a place for you.
John 14:2*

But, as it is written, "What no eye has seen, nor ear heard, nor the heart of man imagined, what God has prepared for those who love him"—1 Corinthians 2:9

Michael Gasaway

Shades of Green

Shades of green she sees all around;
Spring is here and once again her hopes abound.

Could this be the spring that once again she feels love?
This is her prayer that she prays each night above.

How she prays that into her life will ride the man of her dreams;
A real man that really is all that he seems.

One of those men of velvet and steel that she once read;
Do they still exist or just a cowgirls dream dancing in her head.

Then one day he rode into her view;
Oh my, she thought, he is just too good to be true.

They met and the chemistry between them did ignite;
Now together they ride across the pastures under a star filled night.

Don't give up on that dream and that it will happen one day;
Your cowboys horse may have just thrown a shoe so that's why the delay.

So keep hope in your heart and your dreams alive;
Just keep trusting in God above and He will provide.

~~~

I can do all this through him who gives me strength.
Philippians 4:13

And let us not grow weary of doing good, for in due season we will reap, if we do not give up. Galatians 6:9

For with God nothing shall be impossible. Luke 1:37

And now these three remain: faith, hope and love. But the greatest of these is love. 1 Corinthians 13:13

For I know the plans I have for you, declares the Lord, plans for welfare and not for evil, to give you a future and a hope.

For, lo, the winter is past, the rain is over and gone; The flowers appear on the earth; the time of the singing of birds is come, and the voice of the turtle is heard in our land;
Song of Solomon 2:11-12

Delight thyself also in the LORD: and he shall give thee the desires of thine heart. Psalm 37:4

For where your treasure is, there will your heart be also.
Matthew 6:21

A man's heart deviseth his way: but the LORD directeth his steps.
Proverbs 16:9

Michael Gasaway

Hope and Peace

The sunlight caused her blue eyes to sparkle beneath the fall Tennessee sky;
Watching her horses run across the pasture, she sometimes wondered why?

She had faced many challenges, changes and trials over the years;
This year however seemed to bring out her fears along with even more tears.

Going on each day doing the best she could, just to get by and go on;
Sometimes sleep didn't come as she just anxiously waited for the dawn.

Her love of music seemed to offer her no consolation or happiness as it once had;
Trying to write, play or sing just seemed to bring back memories making her even more sad.

How long would this last and deeper into depression must she fall;
Facing this struggle and mounting stress she just went forward giving her all.

Then one day she read a story in a book that as a gift she had received;
It seemed to offer her hope and peace and again started making her believe.

Slowly the change started coming over her and then opened her eyes to really see;
Back to church and reading the Bible she began understanding God's grace was hers to receive.

Brighter days have come upon her and she feels are here to stay;
That special cowboy had come back into her life that she had once sent away.

That cowboy seems to have brought her brighter days and passionate nights;
She awakens now with a smile on her face with a heart filled with such delight.

So never give up on your dreams or let despair keep you knocked down and win;
Keep trusting in God above believing and knowing that He will give you the desires of your heart in the end.

~~~

Rejoicing in hope; patient in tribulation; remaining constant in prayer; Romans 12:12

The righteous cry, and the LORD heareth, and delivereth them out of all their troubles. The LORD is nigh unto them that are of a broken heart; and saveth such as be of a contrite spirit. Psalm 34:17-18

May the God of hope fill you with all joy and peace in believing, so that by the power of the Holy Spirit you may abound in hope. Romans 15:13

For I know the plans I have for you, declares the Lord, plans for welfare and not for evil, to give you a future and a hope. Jeremiah 29:11

Delight thyself also in the LORD: and he shall give thee the desires of thine heart. Commit thy way unto the LORD; trust also in him; and he shall bring it to pass. Psalm 37:4-5

And let us not grow weary of doing good, for in due season we will reap, if we do not give up. Galatians 6:9
For I know the plans I have for you, declares the Lord, plans for welfare and not for evil, to give you a future and a hope. Jeremiah 29:11

Michael Gasaway

Chasing Her Dreams

The memories of him seemed to drift away into the autumn breeze;
Floating off like the brightly colored leaves from the trees.

Time had slowly moved on and now so has she;
It took some time and God's help for her to finally feel free.

The battle in her heart and mind she had finally won;
Now it was time to move on and again start having some fun.

She now awakens each day with a smile on her lovely face;
Believing and knowing that God will see her through with His amazing grace.

Her dreams have been rekindled and her faith is so alive;
Into tomorrow chasing her dreams she does ride.

Finally putting the past behind her as she knows that is where it must stay;
Having learned the lessons she knows that tomorrow will be a brighter day.

Never give up your dreams or the desires of your heart;
Do your best each day and God will always do His part.

So sit tall in the saddle and ride boldly into tomorrow chasing your dreams;
Your destiny, hope and future await you, and are closer than it seems.

∾∾∾

Delight yourself in the Lord, and he will give you the desires of your heart.
Psalm 37:4

Commit your way to the Lord; trust in him, and he will act.
Psalm 37:5

For where your treasure is, there your heart will be also.
Matthew 6:21

The plans of the heart belong to man, but the answer of the tongue is from the Lord. All the ways of a man are pure in his own eyes, but the Lord weighs the spirit. Commit your work to the Lord, and your plans will be established.
Proverbs 16:1-3

He heals the brokenhearted and binds up their wounds.
Psalm 147:3

For he will command his angels concerning you to guard you in all your ways. Psalm 91:11

And let us not grow weary of doing good, for in due season we will reap, if we do not give up.
Galatians 6:9

Michael Gasaway

The Old Ways

The 'Old Ways' are better a lot of us begin to believe;
As the pace of life quickens and all around us, change is all we see.

It's not that change is bad or that I'm against all these new ways;
But why do all the old ways have to be lost to make room for a new day.

With each generation and in every culture it's all the same;
We look back on the old ways with fondness and wonder of them what became.

Some people try to revive these ways or keep them alive from the start;
Wouldn't it be better not to lose what gave us our true heart?

After all isn't that what it's all about, the heart of a nation or its people within;
The old ways should always be preserved and kept like a trusted friend.

Like a friend you can have more than one as you go through life;
Your views can be different but you coexist together without any strife.

Why is it that when it comes to progress and doings things new;
We must do away with the old ways that got our fathers through.

It's when we get into trouble and were faced with a lack;
Remembering of how it was and were always drawn back.

Before it's too late and the old ways are remembered no more;
Do your best now to keep them alive or they will become mere folk lore.

Various ways can be written in a book and passed down the line;
Other ways are more complex and need to be preserved as they are for all time.

Sometimes more important than the actual way;
Is the reason behind why they did something a certain way, back in the day.

Next time you're faced with a choice and an old way will be lost forever;
Ask yourself if tomorrow your children will really be living any better.

Change can be good and on that we must all agree;
But there is always a price to pay and sometimes it's too high when we finally see.

So remember the old ways and try to keep them if you can;
If not they will fade away forever like grains of blowing sand.

∼∼∼

Now I commend you because you remember me in everything and maintain the traditions even as I delivered them to you. 1 Corinthians 11:2

An intelligent heart acquires knowledge, and the ear of the wise seeks knowledge. Proverbs 18:15

*I remember the days of old; I meditate on all that you have done; I ponder the work of your hands.
Psalm 143:5*

Michael Gasaway

Westward Bound

People don't comprehend when I tell them that back out west I must go;
They will never really appreciate it and just will never know.

More than a feeling it's a life style and a way of living life each day;
I try to explain but they don't seem to understand the words I say.

Not just a place on the map that you try to find;
It's truly more than just a place; it's also a state of mind.

From the plains and hill country of Texas that I dearly love;
To those Rocky Mountain States whose snow covered peaks soar above.

From burning deserts, raging rivers to trees that touch the sky;
Wildlife is an everyday occurrence as eagles soar though the crystal blue sky.

Seeing a cactus rose or Texas bluebonnets in the spring all around;
Maybe hiking through an alpine meadow in August with snow still on the ground.

Just like being back home for me when back out west I do roam;
The west for me will always be my home sweet home.

Soon I hope and pray that westward bound I'll be again one day;
Then forever more I'll live in peace and never again to stray.

~~~

For I know the thoughts that I think toward you, saith the LORD, thoughts of peace, and not of evil, to give you an expected end. Jeremiah 29:11

For still the vision awaits its appointed time; it hastens to the end— it will not lie. If it seems slow, wait for it; it will surely come; it will not delay. Habakkuk 2:3

The LORD will perfect that which concerned me: thy mercy, O LORD, endureth for ever: forsake not the works of thine own hands. Psalm 138:8

Commit to the LORD whatever you do, and he will establish your plans. Proverbs 16:3

Delight thyself also in the LORD: and he shall give thee the desires of thine heart. Psalm 37:4

Commit thy way unto the LORD; trust also in him; and he shall bring it to pass. Psalm 37:5

For where your treasure is, there will your heart be also. Matthew 6:21

By faith he went to live in the land of promise.... Hebrews 11:9

Delight yourself in the Lord, and he will give you the desires of your heart. Psalm 37:4

Michael Gasaway

Dedicated to My Grandmother

K'unši

Once she had roamed free across the plains;
Now she was within four walls and given a white man's name.

Assimilation was what the government had called it;
But those that lived through it saw no real benefit.

No longer able to speak her native tongue she had learned;
The white man's language she was taught but freedom she yearned.

It was during the Wetú moon she decided to escape her ordeal;
Down to the river and hide aboard a paddle wheel.

She stole away in the dead of night aboard the ole river boat;
Not realizing it then of the journey embarked upon as down the river she did float.

The years swept by and with Buffalo Bills Wild West show she did go;
Traveling around the country with the troupe doing show after show.

Riding and shooting as well as any man in the west;
The many stories she told me at her knee I can attest.

Stories of the river and when the west was still somewhat wild;
Oh how I loved to hear those stories when I was a child.

My K'unši has longed since passed on but her stories I remember so well;
They live forever in my memory and go around like the carousel in the story she once did tell.

∼∼∼

*I can do all things through Christ which strengthened me.
Philippians 4:13*

Do not be anxious about anything, but in everything by prayer and supplication with thanksgiving let your requests be made known to God. Philippians 4:6

*Beloved, think it not strange concerning the fiery trial which is to try you, as though some strange thing happened unto you:
1 Peter 4:12*

*"How can you say, 'We are wise, and the law of the Lord is with us'? But behold, the lying pen of the scribes has made it into a lie.
Jeremiah 8:8*

Proverbs 16:9 A man's heart deviseth his way: but the L<small>ORD</small> directeth his steps. Proverbs 16:9

And let us not grow weary of doing good, for in due season we will reap, if we do not give up. Galatians 6:9

For with God nothing shall be impossible. Luke 1:37

*For I know the thoughts that I think toward you, saith the L<small>ORD</small>, thoughts of peace, and not of evil, to give you an expected end.
Jeremiah 29:11*

But you, take courage! Do not let your hands be weak, for your work shall be rewarded." 2 Chronicles 15:7 ESV

Michael Gasaway

Mountain Man

Out across the valley he looks at the mountains to the west;
Thinking back and remembering when he began this quest.

A fool's errand some said to him, that's all it would be;
But to him in those mountains he could at last be free.

A stranger and a pilgrim was he to this strange and wondrous land;
To live or die, it would be by his wits and his own hand.

Of the mountain men he learned of their trades;
From the Indians they had taught him their mysterious ways.

As he gazed out and took in all that he could see;
He was still amazed at this marvelous and beautiful wild country.

In his heart he knew that this was where he now belonged;
For a lost love and his past life no longer did he long.

Peace within is what he had sought when he began;
What he found was inside of him resided a true Mountain Man.

This man followed his dreams and found a new life;
Sometimes you just need to put the past behind you along with the strife.

Just over that next mountain is your destiny along with all your dreams;
Now boldly go and seek out your future as it's a lot closer than it seems.

~~~

Angels and Cowboys

∼∼∼

For still the vision awaits its appointed time; it hastens to the end—it will not lie. If it seems slow, wait for it; it will surely come; it will not delay. Habakkuk 2:3

For I know the plans I have for you," declares the LORD, "plans to prosper you and not to harm you, plans to give you hope and a future. Jeremiah 29:11

Listen to advice and accept instruction, that you may gain wisdom in the future. Proverbs 19:20

Delight thyself also in the LORD: and he shall give thee the desires of thine heart. Psalm 37:4

If possible, so far as it depends on you, live peaceably with all. Romans 12:18

Better is a dry morsel with quiet than a house full of feasting with strife. Proverbs 17:1

And we know that all things work together for good to them that love God, to them who are the called according to his purpose. Romans 8:28

And let us not grow weary of doing good, for in due season we will reap, if we do not give up. Galatians 6:9

Michael Gasaway

Mothers Day

They come in all shapes, sizes and colors and love you like no other;
Each has earned and proudly wears the title, Mother.

Always on their mind, in their prayers and forever in their hearts you will stay;
This is how it will always be for them, forever and a day.

When you were but a child they carried you all about;
To the whole world their love for you they wanted to shout.

With you they have always been through thick and thin;
They were with you when your first broken heart they tried to mend.

Their pride for you has never and will never diminish;
They will always be there to help and cheer you on to finish.

Sometimes it seemed they tried to hold on too tight;
But then there were those times you would still cry for them late at night.

You owe them a great debt that you can never ever really repay;
So just remember to call and say; I Love You each day.

You will never really know or understand the sacrifices they made for you along the way;
Unless you too become a Mother and then you will truly realize what they did for you one day.

So never let moments pass you by whether you're young or old to let them know;
As they never grow tired of hearing I Love You, I'm told,

Those three simple words along with a card can mean the world to some;
Now add candy and flowers and a favorite daughter or son you have just become.

Thank them and say a prayer for your Mom each and every day;
After all it was yours Mothers prayers that got you through the hardships along the way.

It seems after all that they have done and been through for you;
To honor and praise them on Mother's Day is the least you can do.

Mom, I couldn't have made it without you along Life's Highway and it seems so little to say;
But thank you for everything, I Love You so very much and oh by the way…..Happy Mother's Day!

~~~

Strength and dignity are her clothing, and she laughs at the time to come. She opens her mouth with wisdom, and the teaching of kindness is on her tongue. She looks well to the ways of her household and does not eat the bread of idleness. Her children rise up and call her blessed; her husband also, and he praises her: "Many women have done excellently, but you surpass them all." ... Proverbs 31:25-30

Honour thy father and thy mother: that thy days may be long upon the land which the LORD thy God giveth thee. Exodus 20:12

Listen, my son, to your father's instruction and do not forsake your mother's teaching. Proverbs 1:8

I have no greater joy than to hear that my children are walking in the truth. 3 John 1:4

Michael Gasaway

Occupies Her Life and Heart

Her life had not been easy from the very start;
She never really knew a mother's love within her heart.

Kids can be so cruel when you feel different and so alone;
It's even worse when there is no one to love you at home.

Then came the time for her to truly be out on her own;
And to look for the love as a child she had never known.

Harder still to find real love when you really never felt it before;
All she wanted was to find love and someone she could also adore.

Sometimes things in life don't go as we plan;
In a few years, she found herself alone again, gone was the man.

Raising her kids and doing all that needed to be done;
There was really never any time for her and any fun.

The kids grew up and moved away, now is her time she thought one day;
Yes time for her to have some fun and maybe even watch a band play.

Things then changed as in life they so often do;
Now taking care of her granddaughter was a priority and a real life rescue.

Back again to raising another child all on her own;
Cowgirl Up she thought, she would not by life be thrown.

That little Indian princess now occupies her life and heart;
Vowing to give her the best life she can and from her to never depart.

No regrets or a worry, just living life to its fullest each day;
Trusting in God and having faith, she knows is the only way.

Raising her up so that with horses and people alike she can survive;
Each day, vowing to give her a better life so that she can truly thrive.

Giving completely of one's self is the best any us can really aspire;
I pray that for each of them, God will grant their hearts desire.

∼∼∼

I am reminded of your sincere faith, a faith that dwelt first in your grandmother Lois and your mother Eunice and now, I am sure, dwells in you as well.
2 Timothy 1:5

"Only take care, and keep your soul diligently, lest you forget the things that your eyes have seen, and lest they depart from your heart all the days of your life. Make them known to your children and your children's children—
Deuteronomy 4:9

Train up a child in the way he should go; even when he is old he will not depart from it. Proverbs 22:6

Grandchildren are the crown of the aged, and the glory of children is their fathers. Proverbs 17:6

Michael Gasaway

A Shooting Star

Standing on the edge of the lake watching the setting of the sun;
Thinking back she wonders how it had all come undone.

Sometimes things happen in life that seems to be out of your control;
The pain we feel seems to touch us deep into our very soul.

That is how it was for her at this time in her life;
She couldn't remember a time when she had felt this much strife.

This past year had brought more pain and suffering than she had ever known in her past;
At times she wondered just how long all this physical and emotional turmoil would last.

A shooting star caught her eye as it flashed across the ebony sky;
In that moment she realized it was time to grab hold of life's reins and ride cowgirl ride.

Time to put the past away where it really belonged;
Move on into tomorrow seeking those dreams she had so longed.

Years have gone by and her heart and body has healed within;
Remembering back to that shooting star and when she decided to begin again.

Now her future is brighter than she has ever thought it could be;
All it took was for her to perceive what she really wanted and then just believe.

Never give up on your dreams or the desires of your heart;
Each day is a new beginning and for you a brand new start.

So start each day with a song in your heart and a smile on your face;
Let God lead guide and direct your steps with His unconditional love and amazing grace.

∼∼∼

Now when these things begin to take place, straighten up and raise your heads, because your redemption is drawing near." Luke 21:28

Delight yourself in the Lord, and he will give you the desires of your heart.
Commit your way to the Lord; trust in him, and he will act.
Psalm 37:4-5

And let us not grow weary of doing good, for in due season we will reap, if we do not give up. Galatians 6:9

For with God nothing shall be impossible. Luke 1:37

Be ye strong therefore, and let not your hands be weak: for your work shall be rewarded.
2 Chronicles 15:7

Rejoice evermore. Pray without ceasing. In everything give thanks: for this is the will of God in Christ Jesus concerning you. 1 Thessalonians 5:16-18

And we know that all things work together for good to them that love God, to them who are the called according to his purpose. Romans 8:28

But Jesus looked at them and said, "With man this is impossible, but with God all things are possible." Matthew 19:26

Fear not, for I am with you; be not dismayed, for I am your God; I will strengthen you, I will help you, I will uphold you with my righteous right hand. Isaiah 41:10

Again Jesus spoke to them, saying, "I am the light of the world. Whoever follows me will not walk in darkness, but will have the light of life." John 8:12

Have not I commanded thee? Be strong and of a good courage; be not afraid, neither be thou dismayed: for the LORD thy God is with thee whithersoever thou goest. Joshua 1:9

Michael Gasaway

Life's Dance

The moon glistened off her dark hair like an eagle's wing in flight;
Her azure blue eyes seem to sparkle and dance as they are touched by the full moons light.

Would this be the year her one special dream might come true;
She had kept her faith but felt this one dream was long overdue.

This dream was simple in her mind as dreams go it seems;
Finding that one special cowboy and to share each other's dreams.

Many "cowboys" she had met over time as the years had gone by;
But none could ever measure up although one did try.

In her mind it didn't seem all that hard to measure up and love her for all her days;
A real cowboy to be her friend and lover and could understand her cowgirl ways.

Then as if on cue or ordained from heaven above on that star filled night;
She met a handsome cowboy who tipped his hat and spoke words that made her feel so right.

They sat and talked of their lives both present and the past;
Of love and life, of plans and dreams and the ones that didn't last.

The years have moved on and back to ole' Ft Worth town they sometimes go;
To celebrate their meeting and the true love that does between them still flow.

So never give up on your dreams or the desires of your heart;
Never settle or lower your standards and let God do his part.

One day it will all come to pass and a bright future you will see;
Just keep trusting in God and believe and in life's dance always let God lead.

∾∾∾

So faith comes from hearing, and hearing through the word of Christ. Romans 10:17

"And whatever you ask in prayer, you will receive, if you have faith." Matthew 21:22

Delight yourself in the Lord, and he will give you the desires of your heart. Commit your way to the Lord; trust in him, and he will act. Psalm 37:4-5

Set me as a seal upon your heart, as a seal upon your arm, for love is strong as death, jealousy is fierce as the grave. Its flashes are flashes of fire, the very flame of the Lord. Many waters cannot quench love, neither can floods drown it. Song of Solomon 8:6-7

Ecclesiastes 3:4-5, 7-8 To everything there is a season, and a time to every purpose under the heaven: , and a time to dance; a time to embrace, and a time to refrain from embracing; A time to rend, and a time to sew; a time to keep silence, and a time to speak; A time to love....

Trust in the Lord with all your heart, and do not lean on your own understanding. In all your ways acknowledge him, and he will make straight your paths. Proverbs 3:5-6

Casting all your anxieties on him, because he cares for you. 1 Peter 5:7

Michael Gasaway

Hopes and Dreams

Her emerald green eyes sparkled like the stars on a bright Texas night;
Shimmering like spun gold her blonde hair glistened in the full moons light.

Twenty some years had gone by and her decision was now made;
No longer would she allow herself to be an abused slave.

Abuse in not just physical as many may believe in life;
Verbal abuse with words can cause equal stress and seems to cut like a knife.

The pain inflected in this manner, sometimes takes even longer to heal;
It may not be physical but is just as hurtful and so very real.

Just because it's not visible to others that each day you may meet;
That doesn't mean it doesn't exist with pain and scars kept way down deep.

Now it was time for her to move on and to seek out and follow her dream;
Little did she know or realize that it was closer than it seemed.

This cowboy she had just met was so different than anyone she had ever known;
His words seemed to touch her heart and soul more than she had ever been shown.

Words that he spoke gave her hope and peace in the decision she had made;
He made her laugh and smile and she found herself no longer leery or afraid.

Helping her to move forward in life, slowly she began to feel and heal;
No longer did she think that her thoughts and words she had to conceal.

Time slowly moved on as they became closer with each passing day;
Together now their lives move forward and seem to just flow, as if in some magical ballet.

Don't let abuse physically or verbally cause you any more strife and pain;
Seek help today so that your hopes and dreams you will one day attain.

∼∼∼

Let your speech always be gracious, seasoned with salt, so that you may know how you ought to answer each person. Colossians 4:6

"For by your words you will be justified, and by your words you will be condemned." Matthew 12:37

Let no corrupting talk come out of your mouths, but only such as is good for building up, as fits the occasion, that it may give grace to those who hear. Ephesians 4:29

Cast out the scorner, and contention shall go out; yea, strife and reproach shall cease. Proverbs 22:10

To slander no one, to be peaceable and considerate, and always to be gentle toward everyone. Titus 3:2

Do not let any unwholesome talk come out of your mouths, but only what is helpful for building others up according to their needs, that it may benefit those who listen. Ephesians 4:29

And the God of all grace, who called you to his eternal glory in Christ, after you have suffered a little while, will himself restore you and make you strong, firm and steadfast. 1 Peter 5:10

Do you see someone who speaks in haste? There is more hope for a fool than for them. Proverbs 29:20

Take delight in the LORD, and he will give you the desires of your heart. Commit your way to the LORD; trust in him and he will do this: Psalm 37:4-5

Trust in the Lord with all your heart, and do not lean on your own understanding. Proverbs 3:5

Michael Gasaway

River of Love

Watching the full moon rise over the tall peaks towering high above;
His thoughts turned back to her and their time together along the river of love.

It had only been a short time since they met on that star filled Austin night;
They had found a love with one another that seemed to feel so right.

Happening so fast between them, as true love often does it seems;
Love at first sight, just like watching a movie up on the wide screen.

Sometimes in life love touches us softly like the wing of a turtledove;
Then there are times that it strikes us like lighting from above.

On this night away from her, his thoughts turned to her once again;
Thinking back to that Texas Hill Country weekend and how it did begin.

Oh how those days of summer were hot and the nights hotter still;
The closer they became in this special love so true and very real.

Now remembering those days they spent together walking hand n' hand;
And of that special time together along the Frio River in Concan.

The mountains they climbed and the closeness they grew along the way;
They shared with each other the stories of their past lives as they climbed along that day.

Around the campfire each night the embers seemed to dance high into the sky;
They held each other close and danced along the river as their love did intensify.

Yes a Cowboy and a Texas Angel fell in love along the river that summer eve;

Now they ride together side by side and in true love they now believe.

~~~

Love is patient and kind. Love is not jealous or boastful or proud or rude. It does not demand its own way. It is not irritable, and it keeps no record of being wronged. It does not rejoice about injustice but rejoices whenever the truth wins out. Love never gives up, never loses faith, is always hopeful, and endures through every circumstance. Prophecy and speaking in unknown languages and special knowledge will become useless. But love will last forever!
1 Corinthians 13:4-8

Delight yourself in the Lord, and he will give you the desires of your heart. Psalm 37:4

And let us not grow weary of doing good, for in due season we will reap, if we do not give up. Galatians 6:9

Beloved, let us love one another, for love is from God, and whoever loves has been born of God and knows God.
1 John 4:7

Michael Gasaway

Majestic Creatures

They are majestic creatures that God created for us to love;
One look in their eyes and you know they were sent from up above.

They will love you in that unconditional sort of way;
And all they want in return is a little of your time and some hay.

I speak of the horse and of that you may not understand;
Unless you have ridden one across this great land.

They come in all sizes and colors, like people it seems;
To have one as a child had always been a dream.

Once you come to know these creatures as I have done;
You will never be the same and will always want to be around one.

To ride across the pasture and feel the wind on your face;
Now that is just part of Gods amazing grace.

It's like no other feeling that I can describe;
Making you feel free and alive anytime you go out for a ride.

It may be across the desert while in bloom or along the beach;
Any place you can ride is like having heaven within your reach

So next time a horse you happen to see;
Thank God for creating these Majestic Creatures, just for you and me.

∼∼∼

The horse is made ready for the day of battle, but the victory belongs to the Lord. Proverbs 21:31

If we put bits into the mouths of horses so that they obey us, we guide their whole bodies as well.
James 3:3

Their horses are swifter than leopards, more fierce than the evening wolves; their horsemen press proudly on. Their horsemen come from afar; they fly like an eagle swift to devour.
Habakkuk 1:8

For it is by grace you have been saved, through faith—and this is not from yourselves, it is the gift of God—not by works, so that no one can boast. Ephesians 2:8-9

Love bears all things, believes all things, hopes all things, endures all things. 1 Corinthians 13:7 ESV

The horse is made ready for the day of battle, but the victory belongs to the Lord. Proverbs 21:31

"Then loud beat the horses' hoofs with the galloping, galloping of his steeds." Judges 5:22

Michael Gasaway

I Choose You

I choose you were the words that he had said;
Why then within her heart was she feeling a certain amount of dread?

Yet inside her heart she felt both happy and sad;
Something deep within told her however that this could only end bad.

We all want to be chosen by someone in life that is true;
But if it's between two loves then someone will be left broken and blue.

Our lives are made up by the choices that we make and say;
They can take you forward toward happiness or lead you astray.

Choose ever so wisely each decision you make in life;
For if you choose without God you'll likely be faced with more than just strife.

Don't put yourself into a situation that you're a choice someone has to make;
Better to be alone and move on in life and that person forsake.

Let God be your guide and lead your steps each day;
Then you won't ever wonder about the words that they say.

Sometimes she thinks back to that time long ago;
And thanks God that she did listen and just let him go.

God will always speak to you about the decisions that you need to make;
You just need to be open and listen before the road you take.

Now she has met the love of her life and is happier than ever before;
She has learned now to just let God and allow Him to lead her through each of life's doors.

~~~

Trust in the Lord with all your heart, and do not lean on your own understanding. In all your ways acknowledge him, and he will make straight your paths.
Proverbs 3:5-6

If any of you lack wisdom, let him ask of God, that giveth to all men liberally, and upbraideth not; and it shall be given him.
James 1:5

For I know the plans I have for you, declares the Lord, plans for welfare and not for evil, to give you a future and a hope.
Jeremiah 29:11

All scripture is given by inspiration of God, and is profitable for doctrine, for reproof, for correction, for instruction in righteousness: 2 Timothy 3:16

Seek the Lord and his strength, seek his face continually.
1 Chronicles 16:11

Michael Gasaway

This was written and dedicated to my Dad and all fathers out there for Father's Day. Reach out today and give your dad a call if you can. If not lift up a prayer for him and let him know, that you still do care and miss him so.

My Dad

He was born on the wide Oklahoma plains;
The blood of Lakota warriors he had coursing through his veins.

A man's man was he that can truly be said;
As hard as nails was he, but never so hard not to bow his head.

Serving in WWII, Korea and Vietnam;
It was he that helped to make me the man that I am.

The shooting medals on his chest were gold;
As he was one of the best shots in the Corps, I'm told.

Standing tall in his dress blues with rows of medals and gold wings upon his chest;
My Dad was one of our nation's best.

Raised up a family with his wife and had two sons;
Teaching us to always do what is right and to follow the Son.

I learned respect from him and how to fish and shoot;
To him it was that I gave my first salute.

Taught me pride in God, family, country and the Corps;
And to always do my best at any given chore.

On this Father's day and every day I pay him the respect he is due;
Dad I will always love and be so proud of you.

Semper Fi Dad, with Fair Winds and Following Seas;
Hope you look down and are proud of the man I turned out to be.

Lift up a prayer for fathers out there every where today;
Tell him you love them and for them always pray.

~~~

As a father shows compassion to his children, so the LORD shows compassion to those who fear him.
Psalms 103:13

Children, obey your parents in the Lord, for this is right. Honor your father and mother, that it may go well with you and that you may live long in the land.
Ephesians 6:1-3

Grandchildren are the crown of the aged, and the glory of children is their fathers. Proverbs 17:6

Honour thy father and thy mother: that thy days may be long upon the land which the LORD thy God giveth thee. Exodus 20:12

My son, hear the instruction of thy father…..
Proverbs 1:8

Michael Gasaway

Roosevelt's Rough Riders

From all around the west down to ole San Antone' they came;
They came to serve and not for fortune or fame.

They were cowboys, Indians, buffalo soldiers, gamblers and men looking for adventure;
Together they all came to Texas for a call of duty to answer.

Across from the Alamo in the Menger hotel they gathered to sign;
Then out to Ft. Sam Houston to become military aligned.

Blue flannel shirts, brown trousers, slouch hats; a polka dot handkerchief was their uniform;
Into Roosevelt's Rough Riders they did transform.

Traveling on to Florida by train to await a boat;
Then on to Cuba where the Spanish they hoped to smote.

In early afternoon up Kettle Hill the Rough Riders advanced under heavy fire;
They overcame the Spanish as had been their desire.

TR pressed on the assault to acquire San Juan Heights as was his plan;
Hundreds of rough Riders charged up the hill fighting hand to hand.

July 1, 1898 was the date that went down in history;
The day a future president led his men into battle and on to victory.

Men like TR seem to be far and few in this modern age we live;
Those that fought for right and freedom and could also be decisive.

Let us pray that another true leader will lead our country once again;
Someone that will put us on the right track and take us out of this deadly tailspin.

~~~

A time to love, and a time to hate; a time of war, and a time of peace. Ecclesiastes 3:8

And the angel of the Lord appeared to him and said to him, "The Lord is with you, O mighty man of valor." Judges 6:12

Blessed be the Lord my strength which teaches my hands to war, and my fingers to fight: Psalm 144:1

Even though I walk through the valley of the shadow of death, I will fear no evil, for you are with me; your rod and your staff, they comfort me. Psalms 23:4

Thou art my battle axe and weapons of war: for with thee will I break in pieces the nations, and with thee will I destroy kingdoms; Jeremiah 51:20

It is joy to the just to do judgment: but destruction shall be to the workers of iniquity. Proverbs 21:15

Michael Gasaway

Pay it Forward

Times were tough for her and money was tight;
On to her next job before she could call it a night.

Stopping here once in awhile was such a treat;
Remembering the many times together here they did eat.

She was thinking of him as she waited in line at Chick-fil-a;
Happy memories they had shared together in her mind did replay.

Reaching the window she started to hand the money to pay;
The young man said, "Your bill has already been paid today."

"The driver ahead of you paid it forward with these words he did say";
"Tell her God is with her and to have a blessed day."

That small act of kindness changed her life and gave her hope;
Closer to God she was drawn and was given the strength to cope.

Time went by and her future is now brighter than it has ever been;
Often she remembers back to that day and pays it forward again and again.

Now she can afford to help others that may be in need;
Every day now she tries to plant a pay it forward seed.

Sometimes just a small act of generosity can change a life in a day;
You never know the positive affect you have with the blessing you convey.

Your actions and kindness can have a very positive impact on a life;
It may be the only bright spot they see in a life filled with strife.

Just doing a random act of kindness can mean a great deal;
It's not just about buying someone's next meal.

Do something for another with no thought of anything in return;
You will teach a lesson and maybe of God they will learn.

So pay it forward every chance that you have with God's help from above;

God will provide you with opportunities to display His mercy and love.

Make it your mission today to pay it forward when the chance you get;
You'll never look back on that moment with any regret.

~~~

"So whatever you wish that others would do to you, do also to them, for this is the Law and the Prophets. "
Matthew 7:12

And as you wish that others would do to you, do so to them.
Luke 6:31

The second is this: 'You shall love your neighbor as yourself.' There is no other commandment greater than these."
Mark 12:31

Michael Gasaway

Long Live the Cowboy

It was a time of war and each had gone their own way;
One had chosen blue and the other had chosen grey.

Years went by and the many battles they had seen;
In his own way each somehow felt unclean.

Now the war was over and both not realizing it had been at Appomattox that day;
It would be some time until their trails crossed again along the way.

They each had turned their horse west, into the setting sun;
Each was now hoping that they might find some sort absolution.

Finally as fate would have it their trails crossed in a dusty Texas town;
They hugged each other as brothers do; now neither was wearing a frown.

Over drinks of whiskey they talked of the war and battles they were in;
Then they made plans on what to do and how to begin again.

Down to their ranch in south Texas and raise a herd of cattle to sell;
One had heard that those longhorns had thrived while they had both served in hell.

It took some time and every dime they could scrounge together;
Now they headed north a thousand miles to face bandits, Indians and all kinds of weather.

That's just one of the many stories and how it all began;
The cattle drives north that helped feed people across this great land.

Many a ranch in Texas can trace its roots to back after the civil War;
That's when thousands of longhorns were driven north to the closest rail and boxcar.

This was the heyday of the real cowboy and of his glory days;
Now they are distant memories fogged by histories haze.

They still live on today but are few and far between of course;
Not too many left making his way with just a rope and his horse.

They seem now to just survive in stories, art and poems;
Lift up a toast and may long live the Cowboy, wherever he roams.

~~~

*For still the vision awaits its appointed time; it hastens to the end—
it will not lie. If it seems slow, wait for it; it will surely come; it will
not delay. Habakkuk 2:3*

*The Lord will fulfill his purpose for me; your steadfast love, O Lord,
endures forever. Do not forsake the work of your hands.
Psalm 138:8*

*For I know the plans I have for you, declares the Lord, plans for
welfare and not for evil, to give you a future and a hope.
Jeremiah 29:11*

*Trust in the Lord with all your heart, and do not lean on your own
understanding. In all your ways acknowledge him, and he will
make straight your paths.
Proverbs 3:5-6*

Michael Gasaway

Let It Go

She stood at the fence line and watched the sun slowly rise;
Sometimes without realizing it, tears fell from her dazzling green eyes.

When would the pain end and release her from loves chains;
How long before she would be rid of all her past pains.

A love for him she still felt deep in her heart within;
It had been his choice to move on and start anew again.

The reasons never made any since to her, deep in her soul;
When times got tough, you got closer, you didn't just let go.

True love doesn't give up when times get rough;
This is when you come together and face them with love.

He had made the choice alone and sent her on her way;
Now it was time to stop wondering where love had gone each day.

You can't move on in life, if you keep holding onto the past;
It's time to begin again, and find your true love that will last.

It's hard to reach out and receive what God wants to give;
If you're still holding on to the memories of how you use to live.

Let it go and reach forward with both hands as into the future you go;
So that God can lead you and your dreams, He can show.

Tomorrow is yours to claim if you keep the faith and really believe;
Look forward in trust and one day your one true love, you will see.

Never give up and keep moving onward with a smile on your face;
God will always be with you, along with His guidance and grace.

∼∼∼

"Remember not the former things, nor consider the things of old. Behold, I am doing a new thing; now it springs forth, do you not perceive it? I will make a way in the wilderness and rivers in the desert."
Isaiah 43:18-19

Casting all your anxieties on him, because he cares for you.
1 Peter 5:7

Trust in the Lord with all your heart, and do not lean on your own understanding. In all your ways acknowledge him, and he will make straight your paths.
Proverbs 3:5-6

Cast your burden on the Lord, and he will sustain you; he will never permit the righteous to be moved.
Psalm 55:22

Brethren, I do not count myself to have apprehended; but one thing I do, forgetting those things which are behind and reaching forward to those things which are ahead, I press toward the goal for the prize of the upward call of God in Christ Jesus.
Philippians 3:13-14

Michael Gasaway

Into The Future

She took the cross he'd given her down off the wall and put it in a drawer;
It was time for her to move on and not live in the past anymore.

A glass heart filled with love and sand was the next thing that she put away;
There were no more tears to cry and no more words left to say.

Into the future she knew that is where her destiny would be found;
But the memories still flooded back at times and put her in a tailspin around and around.

A year was nearly upon her and she had met someone new;
Why was it then that sometimes she still felt down and blue?

Maybe she thought of the memories she would never really be free;
Only time would really tell if truly free, one day she might be.

Of the love she remembered they had shared had been oh so true and pure;
At times she questions her decision and felt unsure.

Now with her new love she was going forward hand and hand;
The decision had been hers and she had made a final stand.

Why then did his memory still come to her as she held her new love close at night?
One day she hoped that of his memory she'd be free and once again feel right.

Sometimes in life we make decisions' that we have to live with the rest of our days;
You go forward in life and then descending upon you, memories cover your eyes in a haze.

She has resigned herself that into memories she would always look back again;
Their love had been that strong and a part of her would always belong to him.

~~~

Set me as a seal upon your heart, as a seal upon your arm, for love is strong as death, jealousy is fierce as the grave. Its flashes are flashes of fire, the very flame of the Lord. Many waters cannot quench love, neither can floods drown it. If a man offered for love all the wealth of his house, he would be utterly despised.
Song of Solomon 8:6-7

I thank my God upon every remembrance of you,
Philippians 1:3

Trust in the LORD with all thine heart; and lean not unto thine own understanding. In all thy ways acknowledge him, and he shall direct thy paths. Proverbs 3:5-6

If any of you lack wisdom, let him ask of God, that giveth to all men liberally, and upbraideth not; and it shall be given him.
James 1:5

Michael Gasaway

Texas Angel

Typing and talking over the miles the closer they grew;
Each was secretly wondering if what they were feeling was true.

It was only a few days but neither really wanted to wait;
So they decided to meet and see if this was loves fate.

On he drove the many miles on that fateful night;
Then there she stood beneath the Texas stars so bright.

Her blond hair seemed to frame her beautiful face;
Like an angel fair filled with a special grace.

He couldn't believe his eyes as he saw her standing there;
A Texas Angel, whose beauty was beyond compare?

She walked up and kissed him more passionately than he had ever known;
Like the song says, "this ole cowboy had just been thrown".

His heart and head were both now reeling;
Like a school boy he felt from the emotions he was feeling.

He placed his hands gently on her face and looked deep into her soft green eyes.
Then he kissed her back passionately beneath that star filled sky;

She stepped back and flashed him a million dollar smile;
Then motioned with her finger and said, "Come on in cowboy and stay awhile".

Inside the candles were all aglow and the mood was right;
They held each other close as their love grew stronger that night.

A lonesome Cowboy and a Texas Angel met under that star filled sky;
Now together into the sunset they ride forever, side by side.

~~~

For this very night there stood before me an angel of the God to whom I belong and whom I worship, Acts 27:23

*Beloved, let us love one another, for love is from God, and whoever loves has been born of God and knows God.
1 John 4:7*

We love because he first loved us. 1 John 4:19

Let all that you do be done in love. 1 Corinthians 16:14

Let him kiss me with the kisses of his mouth! For your love is better than wine; Song of Solomon 1:2

So now faith, hope, and love abide, these three; but the greatest of these is love. 1 Corinthians 13:13

Delight yourself in the Lord, and he will give you the desires of your heart. Psalm 37:4

And above all these put on love, which binds everything together in perfect harmony. Colossians 3:14

For as he thinketh in his heart, so is he: Proverbs 23:7

Trust in the Lord *with all thine heart; and lean not unto thine own understanding. In all thy ways acknowledge him, and he shall direct thy paths. Proverbs 3:5-6*

Michael Gasaway

The Whiskey

Another drink of whiskey as it seems to dull his pain;
Out on the tin roof he hears the rhythm of the rain.

The rain falls harder now and so does he;
His tears fall faster flowing like a river to the sea.

Deeper into the dark abyss of memories he falls;
There is nothing left to give, he gave her his all.

His spirit inside cries out in turmoil and pain;
"When would it all end, where is the gain?"

"Farewell to thee", he says, "I tried my best";
"With the light of dawn I begin my new life quest."

"You always saw the bad and never the good;
I tried to tell you but you never understood."

The days went by and the years they became;
Then one day out went loves flickering flame.

"I know in the past you had lied and been untrue;
By your side I stood and still loved you."

Then that day finally came that he knew might come;
It was a Saturday when everything just came undone.

"No way could you see a means to save the love we shared;
It seems as if you were possessed and no longer seemed to care."

Now the past is behind him and he has moved on;
No longer is he a slave to his memories or what went wrong.

Now a bright future he has found with a new love in his life;
Never giving up on love and will soon have a devoted and loving wife.

Keep trusting in God and just perceive and believe;
Then one day a bright new future you will also see.

∾∾∾

*That I have great heaviness and continual sorrow in my heart.
Romans 9:2*

They that sow in tears shall reap in joy. Psalm 126:5

And my God will meet all your needs according to the riches of his glory in Christ Jesus. Philippians 4:19

Give, and it will be given to you. Good measure, pressed down, shaken together, running over, will be put into your lap. For with the measure you use it will be measured back to you." Luke 6:38

"Ask, and it will be given to you; seek, and you will find; knock, and it will be opened to you. Matthew 7:7

*For I know the thoughts that I think toward you, saith the LORD, thoughts of peace, and not of evil, to give you an expected end.
Jeremiah 29:11*

*Give strong drink to the one who is perishing, and wine to those in bitter distress; let them drink and forget their poverty and remember their misery no more.
Proverbs 31:6-7*

Do not get drunk on wine, which leads to debauchery. Instead, be filled with the Spirit, Ephesians 5:18

Michael Gasaway

Just Walk Away

Love is like a drug some people say;
And it can be just as addictive in every way.

Like a drug some people are really addicted to love;
They feel all the same things that a real drug does.

Your high on love and everything seems so right;
Then it fades away, leaving you praying for daylight.

I guess it's really like being high on drugs as how it makes you feel;
It's such a euphoric feeling and seems so real.

Then like drugs the feelings seem to die away;
You try to recapture it, but the feelings just slip further each day.

Like drugs coming down from love can be so very hard indeed;
It will sometimes drop you to your knees.

Try as you might nothing seems to work to get them off your mind;
I guess with both, it just takes God and time.

If drugs are bad and love is supposed to be good for you;
Then why do both hurt so much leaving down and blue?

I guess it's as I've heard people talk;
Never need or love something so much that away you can't just walk.

To both it seems sometimes you have to just walk away;
Leave them both behind and start with a brand new day.

It's not an easy thing to do and will test you as it takes its emotional toll;
But walk away sometimes you must, to save your soul.

Then walk into the daylight with your head held high;
This is your day, the beginning of your new life, tell your past goodbye.

~~~

Love is patient and kind; love does not envy or boast; it is not arrogant or rude. It does not insist on its own way; it is not irritable or resentful; it does not rejoice at wrongdoing, but rejoices with the truth. Love bears all things, believes all things, hopes all things, endures all things. Love never ends. As for prophecies, they will pass away; as for tongues, they will cease; as for knowledge, it will pass away.
1 Corinthians 13:4-8

Therefore to him that knoweth to do good, and doeth it not, to him it is sin. James 4:17

Trust in the LORD with all thine heart; and lean not unto thine own understanding. In all thy ways acknowledge him, and he shall direct thy paths. Proverbs 3:5-6

For I know the thoughts that I think toward you, saith the LORD, thoughts of peace, and not of evil, to give you an expected end.
Jeremiah 29:11

Michael Gasaway

A Warrior Once

He kept reaching out in all the ways that he could;
Prayin' that maybe one day the words he spoke would be understood.

To his credit he never gave up and kept trying to reach out;
Sometimes the pain he felt inside was so great he wanted to shout.

He prayed each day that things would change and be better again;
But sometimes the sadness and loss would build up within.

Daily he went about his routine in life with a smile on his face;
Deep within he was just keeping pace in life's race.

The lows and highs he had seen in his lifetime here on earth;
Sometimes he did wonder what had been the good in his birth.

You never know the pain and suffering someone does carry inside;
It's not yours or my place to judge them, who are we to decide.

That old man that you just passed by without a thought or care;
Having been a warrior once and had defended your freedom over there.

Things he had seen in his life would turn most a shade of green;
But his memories of those times had not left him bitter or mean.

Every loss you can think of on his terms he did face;
Thanking God for walking with him and showing His merciful grace.

Now the years seem to speed by for him so fast;
At times he can't help but wonder if this one will be his last.

Death he does not fear as he has faced it so many times in his life;
He'd love to find peace at last without all the heart ache and strife.

Soon off again he will ride into the setting sun;
With a prayer on his lips that he'll find peace before his next day is done.

∼∼∼

And we know that all things work together for good to them that love God, to them who are the called according to his purpose. Romans 8:28

And let us not grow weary of doing good, for in due season we will reap, if we do not give up. Galatians 6:9

For with God nothing shall be impossible. Luke 1:37

*Be ye strong therefore, and let not your hands be weak: for your work shall be rewarded.
2 Chronicles 15:7*

The LORD hears his people when they call to him for help. He rescues them from all their troubles. The LORD is close to the brokenhearted; he rescues those whose spirits are crushed. The righteous person faces many troubles, but the LORD comes to the rescue each time. For the LORD protects the bones of the righteous; not one of them is broken! Psalm 34:17-20

I have said these things to you, that in me you may have peace. In the world you will have tribulation. But take heart; I have overcome the world." John 16:33

Michael Gasaway

Cowboy Up!

In the distance the shadows slowly crept up the tall pines;
Down in the valley below he could hear a coyote whine.

Another long day riding across the mountains heading west;
He could feel the aches and pains and was looking for some rest.

Sitting on a log he gazed up at the stars stretching across the sky;
Sometimes he thought back in time and just wondered why?

The losses seemed to keep mounting up one after another;
He lost his wife, then his son, his father and that one special other.

Some wondered how he had even survived all the losses in his life;
In such a short time how does one survive such strife?

It had taken a tremendous toll on him and this he knew;
Never giving up on himself or God but sometimes feeling blue.

Now he was chasing a dream that had always been in his heart;
This was the time for a new beginning and a fresh start.

His trust in God never wavered and his faith strayed true;
Cowboy up each day as that is what he was always taught to do.

No matter what strife you may face in life, never give up and always believe;
Then one day like this cowboy, your heart's desire you will receive.

~~~

For everything there is a season, and a time for every matter under heaven: a time to be born, and a time to die; a time to plant, and a time to pluck up what is planted; a time to kill, and a time to heal; a time to break down, and a time to build up; a time to weep, and a time to laugh; a time to mourn, and a time to dance; a time to cast away stones, and a time to gather stones together; a time to embrace, and a time to refrain from embracing; ... Ecclesiastes 3:1-8

I can do all things through him who strengthens me.
Philippians 4:13

And let us not grow weary of doing good, for in due season we will reap, if we do not give up. Galatians 6:9

Delight yourself in the Lord, and he will give you the desires of your heart. Psalm 37:4

"Remember not the former things, nor consider the things of old. Behold, I am doing a new thing; now it springs forth, do you not perceive it? I will make a way in the wilderness and rivers in the desert. Isaiah 43:18-19

Cast all your anxiety on him because he cares for you.
1 Peter 5:7

Blessed are they that mourn: for they shall be comforted. Matthew 5:4

Trust in the Lord with all thine heart; and lean not unto thine own understanding. In all thy ways acknowledge him, and he shall direct thy paths. Proverbs 3:5-6

And we know that all things work together for good to them that love God, to them who are the called according to his purpose. Romans 8:28

For I know the plans I have for you," says the Lord. "They are plans for good and not for disaster, to give you a future and a hope. Jeremiah 29:11

Michael Gasaway

No Fear

There she stood on that same ground she had stood in past years;
Falling from her dazzling blue eyes suddenly came the tears.

Standing there and as if on a breeze, the memories came floating back in;
Try as she might her thoughts once again turned to him.

It had been a long time with so many ups and downs along the trail;
Once she vowed to move on and hoped not to fail.

Her future was now looking brighter than it had ever been.
She was wearing a real smile on her beautiful face once again.

In life you have to make choices and stand by that which you choose;
You never know the outcome at the time; win or lose.

Now she had moved on and was happy with the decision she had made;
No longer was she living in love's haze, or looking at a future alone and afraid.

It's never easy to move on into the future and just let go;
Sometimes that's how God will teach us so that we can grow.

Then you will start to grow into the person God has destined you to become;
And start feeling in your heart, a peace, joy and happiness, with a new life rhythm.

Listen to that new song that in your heart you now hear;
Pray for God's guidance and ride into tomorrow with no doubts or fear.

~~~

The Lord is not slow to fulfill his promise as some count slowness, but is patient toward you, not wishing that any should perish, but that all should reach repentance.
2 Peter 3:9

For God hath not given us the spirit of fear; but of power, and of love, and of a sound mind. 2 Timothy 1:7

Above all, taking the shield of faith, wherewith ye shall be able to quench all the fiery darts of the wicked.
Ephesians 6:16

Trust in the LORD with all thine heart; and lean not unto thine own understanding. In all thy ways acknowledge him, and he shall direct thy paths. Proverbs 3:5-6

For I know the thoughts that I think toward you, saith the LORD, thoughts of peace, and not of evil, to give you an expected end.
Jeremiah 29:11

Michael Gasaway

Run to the Roar

Fear had gripped her heart from love's deep pain;
Trying to put her past behind her seemed to be in vain.

Hard as she tried the memories came flooding back in;
All she really wanted was to just begin all over again.

You can't go forward in life if you let fear have control;
You'll only sink deeper into an abyss and never really feel whole.

Put fear, panic and remorse away and with them be done;
Your future will be brighter and will begin with the rising of the sun.

Because running to panic will only cause you to stumble and fall;
You will lose your focus and direction, and it may cost you all.

Go seek your answers and do pray to God above;
He will direct your steps and put you on the path to true love.

Review your course of action with God and decisive be;
It's now time for you to chart a new course and seek out your victory.

Run to the roar and face your fear and no longer be a pawn;
Seek out good council, listen and truly hear and then move on.

Your answers don't lie in anger, regret or the casting of blame;
The truth is within us all and will always burn like an eternal flame.

Use this flame to ignite a spirit of love, faith, happiness and success;
Let it lead you to your victory that lies ahead, always giving it your best.

~~~

Do not be anxious about anything, but in everything by prayer and supplication with thanksgiving let your requests be made known to God .Philippians 4:6

Anxiety in a man's heart weighs him down, but a good word makes him glad. Proverbs 12:25

*Fear not, for I am with you; be not dismayed, for I am your God; I will strengthen you, I will help you, I will uphold you with my righteous right hand.
Isaiah 41:10*

For God gave us a spirit not of fear but of power and love and self-control. 2 Timothy 1:7

*I will instruct you and teach you in the way you should go; I will counsel you with my eye upon you.
Psalm 32:8*

For I know the plans I have for you, declares the Lord, plans for welfare and not for evil, to give you a future and a hope. Jeremiah 29:11

Michael Gasaway

Wild and Free

From the waves lapping upon the islands shore;
Out to the deserts and mountains of the west where eagles soar.

They roam and run wild and free beneath crystal blue skies;
For hundreds of years this is how they spent their lives.

Wild horses and mustangs, oh how they once roamed so free;
I fear however that their days may be numbered as they are not as free and they use to be.

So majestic as they run across this great land;
They once numbered in the thousands and are now but a few to each band.

Why is it that our government and some men seem only to destroy?
Not seeing these majestic creatures for what they are, and finding joy.

Like us they are descendents from many lands and just want to be free to roam;
It seems that the least we can do is leave them alone to run free on what is theirs and our home.

Take some time and really view these beautiful creatures as I have done;
Let us save them now or like the buffalo they may just disappear into a distant setting sun.

~~~

An intelligent heart acquires knowledge, and the ear of the wise seeks knowledge.
Proverbs 18:15

"How can you say, 'We are wise, and the law of the Lord is with us'? But behold, the lying pen of the scribes has made it into a lie.
Jeremiah 8:8

Listen to advice and accept instruction, that you may gain wisdom in the future.
Proverbs 19:20

And let us not grow weary of doing good, for in due season we will reap, if we do not give up. Galatians 6:9

"Then loud beat the horses' hoofs with the galloping, galloping of his steeds."
Judges 5:22

Michael Gasaway

For All Time

Rising early he drove to Memphis from that ole Ft Worth town;
Was this to be the beginning or just another time he was let down?

Pulling into the complex he sat there in his truck wondering about love;
Then he heard a sweet angelic voice asking him to get out of the truck from above.

Getting out of the truck he slowly walked to the entrance where they were to meet;
She came running to him jumping into his arms, almost knocking him off his feet.

Looking deep into her brown eyes with flecks of gold shinning in the light;
They shared that first kiss together and then more passionately as day turned to night.

This cowboy and angel sat and talked of life and loss each had seen in their life;
The many ups and downs, the good and bad and how each had survived life's strife.

Sometimes all of a sudden she would look deep into his eyes and say;
"Smooch break" and start kissing all of his troubles and fears away.

Love struck them both hard on that hot Memphis night, now so far in the past;
They both felt a love so strong, knowing that it was destined to last.

It seemed surreal as it hit them so solid yet so tender and sweet;
Around Memphis she took him greeting with a big smile everyone they met on the street.

Time went on and then down to his ranch in Texas she did come to stay;
Inseparable they became as their love grew stronger with each passing day.

Then one day the doctor did share with them some fearful news;

A cancer they had discovered and must act quickly so as not to lose.

Time went by with surgery, chemo and radiation she had to bear;
By her side he stayed letting her know of his love and seeing to her complete and total care.

A cold December winter day with a sky that was so very blue;
She looked deep into his eyes and her last words were; "I'll always and forever love you… I'll be waiting for you."

A sad story as some may view it as they read these words in rhyme;
But two found a real true love together that will last into eternity and for all time.

∾∾∾

And the LORD God said, It is not good that the man should be alone; I will make him an help mate for him. Genesis 2:18

She is more precious than rubies; nothing you desire can compare with her. Proverbs 3:15

Let him kiss me with the kisses of his mouth! For your love is better than wine; Song of Solomon 1:2

*"He will wipe away every tear from their eyes, and death shall be no more, neither shall there be mourning, nor crying, nor pain anymore, for the former things have passed away."
Revelation 21:4*

*And everyone who lives and believes in me shall never die.
John 11:26*

Love is patient and kind; love does not envy or boast; it is not arrogant or rude. It does not insist on its own way; it is not irritable or resentful; it does not rejoice at wrongdoing, but rejoices with the truth. Love bears all things, believes all things, hopes all things, endures all things. Love never ends. As for prophecies, they will pass away; as for tongues, they will cease; as for knowledge, it will pass away. 1 Corinthians 13:4-8

Michael Gasaway

Just a Memory

Impossible dreams he had dreamt and seen them come to pass;
But the elusive dream of true love never seemed to last.

Alone now he travels down this new road he has found;
Still he feels the emptiness inside with her not around.

But alone he must go, to seek his new destiny along the trail;
It's a shame she had given up on them and let their love fail.

She should of had had more faith and trust in him and God above;
One day she will realize the real cost of living in fear without love.

Knowing that God now has a new plan for him to follow;
So down this road he now travels, no longer to feel hollow.

Knowing that brighter days lie down this new road;
He just keeps putting his trust in God, as only He knows.

His faithfulness He will one day reward he is so sure;
Until then, sometimes his loneliness he will have to endure.

One day soon his mind and heart will be clear again;
That will be the day that his new life does truly begin.

Now he is looking forward to the dawning of that new day;
Free to live and love again, no longer just a memory slave.

Thanking God for showing him the way from up on high;
The journey has been a rough one, of that he won't lie.

Soon the dawn will begin and with it his new destiny;
In his mind she will finally be put away, as just a sad memory.

~~~

For I know the plans I have for you, declares the Lord, plans for welfare and not for evil, to give you a future and a hope. Jeremiah 29:11

For God gave us a spirit not of fear but of power and love and self-control. 2 Timothy 1:7

And without faith it is impossible to please him, for whoever would draw near to God must believe that he exists and that he rewards those who seek him. Hebrews 11:6

"And whatever you ask in prayer, you will receive, if you have faith." Matthew 21:22

Beloved, let us love one another, for love is from God, and whoever loves has been born of God and knows God. 1 John 4:7

Delight yourself in the Lord, and he will give you the desires of your heart. Psalm 37:4

There is no fear in love, but perfect love casts out fear. For fear has to do with punishment, and whoever fears has not been perfected in love. 1 John 4:18

Michael Gasaway

The Ranger

Traveling these many weeks from San Antoine' to this little border town;
He tracked the bandit across Texas for this, the final showdown.

Circle with a star he wore proudly on his chest;
Everyone knew from this, that this lawman was one of Texas' best.

Now he had him cornered and there would be no escape;
One way or the other the bandit was going to pay for his deadly rape.

A more heinous crime the ranger did not know within his heart;
Ending the bandit's life or bringing him in, he would do his part.

Unmercifully the sun was beating down as sweat dripped from his brow;
Fear tried to grip his heart but this he could not allow.

Checking his colt one last time making sure he and it were both ready to go;
Originally set to bring the bandit in, now he was going to send him straight to hell below.

Fast with a gun the bandit's reputation was known far and wide;
The ranger dismissed this from his mind and became steely eyed.

Pulling his Stetson down to block the sun's rays from his eyes;
He adjusted the colt in his holster, the colonel's way for all men to be equalized.

Almost together the shots rang out as smoke filled the air;
Then there was only the ranger, left standing there.

True and faster had been the ranger's gun that day;
Now it was over, justice served and with his life the bandit did pay.

Avenging the death of his wife and his young son was now complete;
Many more outlaws would meet their fate and fall at this rangers feet.

Across Texas he roamed and his reputation did grow by the year;
Brave men like this ranger, made Texas great as they knew no fear.

~~~

When justice is done, it is a joy to the righteous but terror to evildoers. Proverbs 21:15

For the one in authority is God's servant for your good. But if you do wrong, be afraid, for rulers do not bear the sword for no reason. They are God's servants, agents of wrath to bring punishment on the wrongdoer. Romans 13:4

But let judgment run down as waters, and righteousness as a mighty stream. Amos 5:24

"But you, take courage! Do not let your hands be weak, for your work shall be rewarded." 2 Chronicles 15:7

He has told you, O man, what is good; and what does the Lord require of you but to do justice, and to love kindness, and to walk humbly with your God? Micah 6:8

Learn to do well; seek judgment, relieve the oppressed, judge the fatherless, plead for the widow. Isaiah 1:17

Michael Gasaway

A Warriors Song

A warrior's heart is strong and true and filled with the pureness only real passion can bring;
Each day he faces it the same, never questioning.

Preparing for battle each day not knowing what obstacles might cross his way;
Real or imaginary the battle is the same for truth and love each day.

With each sunrise he faces the east to see another day, a new beginning to start;
Only to see it fade away as so many memories deep within his heart.

On he fights and counts the coup in his mind that he has won;
Vanquishing his enemy one by one, and then watching the setting of the sun.

His strength has diminished over the years with the long battles in his mind he's had to fight;
He's grown weary and longs for a happier time but continues on to do what's right.

The drums he can now hear in the distance echoing him to go;
He can feel their beating down deep in his very soul.

Now he knows what he must do for this war at last to be won;
To have that peace of mind and knowing it is finally done.

Driving the stake deep into the ground, the raw hide strap firm against his skin;
He knows that on this day the battle in his soul will come to an end.

He cry's out to his enemy to let them know that he has no fear;
And to let them know, that now he can see his way clear.

Down upon him they now ride, their screams he feels deep within;
As soon as he has finished one another does begin.

The battle rages on and on until only one demon remains for him to slay;

So he knows that this day he will be free either way.

The demon rides hard and fast at him, his arrows fill the air with a whispering sound;
He holds firm as he knows he must stand his ground.

He can feel the many wounds he has suffered during this long battle of his mind;
And hopes and prays that he has the strength to fight on, one last time.

The demon charges and fly's from his horse and their bodies collide;
It's now mortal combat to the very end as this final battle his fate will decide.

They fight on each cutting the other until he drives the knife deep into the demons very soul;
It's now over, ending in the demons final death roll.

The warrior arises weakened by the battle for his soul that has waged on for so very long;
It's now time for him to ride on and once again finally belong.

He gives thanks for surviving the many battles he has fought and won;
Thanks for the strength and courage to at last see it done.

The sun is now setting and a new day soon will follow;
Now he is free to ride on and no longer feel hollow.

God granted him the will and passion to fight on never wavering;
Now on he rides to seek his fate and a warrior's song to sing.

∾∾∾

For we wrestle not against flesh and blood, but against principalities, against powers, against the rulers of the darkness of this world, against spiritual wickedness in high [places].
Ephesians 6:12

Michael Gasaway

Lonely Trail

Someone once asked me how long does the pain and suffering last from this kind of ordeal;
I said it's up to you my friend on how long you wish to grieve and then begin to heal.

Mourning takes different amounts of time depending on the person you lost;
You will find yourself on a rollercoaster of life just being tossed.

Around you go through different stages of mourning as your thrown all about;
Sometimes the pain you feel will be so great you'll just want to shout.

You can't rush the mending as it takes each person a different amount of time;
Each day out of the abyss of loneliness and despair you must continue to climb.

Slowly time will pass as the healing starts to mend your broken heart within;
Then one day the sun will shine on your face and you'll know you're ready to begin again.

Within your soul their memories and they will always be close and never end;
You'll hold on loosely to them as you move forward and continue to mend.

In your heart you will realize that moving on in life is what they would want you to do;
They would want you to be happy again as they know that's what's best for you.

One day your smile will return and you'll feel God's amazing grace;
You'll look forward to your new future and a new life you're now ready to embrace.

So if you find yourself in the grips of this, one of the greatest torments in life;
Keep believing and praying for God's mercy, as He will deliver you from this and all strife.

God will deliver you and give you peace and understanding as you travel down this lonely trail;
Just know that God will carry you through and his love and mercy will never fail.

∾∾∾

And we know that all things work together for good to them that love God, to them who are the called according to his purpose. Romans 8:28

And God shall wipe away all tears from their eyes; and there shall be no more death, neither sorrow, nor crying, neither shall there be any more pain: for the former things are passed away. Revelation 21:4

"Blessed are those who mourn, for they shall be comforted. "Matthew 5:4

I thank my God in all my remembrance of you, always in every prayer of mine for you all making my prayer with joy, Philippians 1:3-5

Fear thou not; for I am with thee: be not dismayed; for I am thy God: I will strengthen thee; yea, I will help thee; yea, I will uphold thee with the right hand of my righteousness. Isaiah 41:10

I have said these things to you, that in me you may have peace. John 16:33

Do not be anxious about anything, but in everything by prayer and supplication with thanksgiving let your requests be made known to God. Philippians 4:6

Now may the Lord of peace himself give you peace at all times in every way. The Lord be with you all. 2 Thessalonians 3:16

Michael Gasaway

The Plan

Many struggles and happy times she has seen in her life;
She is a devoted mother and was once someone's loving wife.

Things changed for her as she traveled down life's road;
Sometimes it was her choice and other times by what she was told.

Each day she did her best but many times forgot to stop and pray;
Then when she was faced with a choice, she lost her way.

For awhile things seemed to go well and she was even happy for a time;
Then her whole world started to fall apart and completely unwind.

At these times she often cried out to God and asked why me?
Not remembering the choices of her past now put her heart in agony.

From the very beginning God gave us the free will to choose;
Leaving our choices up to us and whether we would win or lose.

You see God has a plan for your life, but the devil does too;
Which one you choose, God leaves that up to you.

The devil's plan seems to give us what at the time appears to be right;
God's plan sometimes can be harder, but in the end your future will be bright.

If guilt and memories convict the choices you have made along the way;
Maybe it's God nudging you and trying to direct your steps this day.

Just open your eyes to see, He's trying to show you which way to go;
He's asking you to put your trust in Him and to always follow.

It's the choices we make in life that can alter the course we take;
Each day your life will be changed by the decisions that you make.

So make your choices wisely and never without thoughtful prayer;
Always pray and allow God to be your most important advisor.

He will always lead and guide you in your life to what is best;
Your actions and not God is what will place you in another of life's test.

Be always in prayer and let God's word be your guide;
Lift up your prayers daily to God, as you look up towards the sky.

Thank God each day for your blessings, even those that you have yet to see;
Let God always guide your steps, and always pray, believe and be ready to receive.

∾∾∾

Put on the full armor of God, so that you can take your stand against the devil's schemes. Ephesians 6:11

Blessed is the man who remains steadfast under trial, for when he has stood the test he will receive the crown of life, which God has promised to those who love him. James 1:12

For I know the thoughts that I think toward you, saith the Lord, thoughts of peace, and not of evil, to give you an expected end. Jeremiah 29:11

You need to persevere so that when you have done the will of God, you will receive what he has promised. Hebrews 10:36

Michael Gasaway

Vaya con Dios, mi Amor

Sometimes things happen in this life and leave you wondering why?
But I know that I can't give up, I must continue on and try.

When she came into my life I was feeling pretty low;
Believing in me and helping to show me the true way that I should go.

Into my life she brought sunshine where there had been storms and strife;
Helping me to grow but alas, was not meant to be my wife.

She helped me to understand His word and brought me closer to Him;
For that I will always be thankful, knowing that the pain was worth it in the end.

I don't understand His ways and they are still a mystery to me;
But her love and friendship were no mystery, and thankful to her and God I will always be.

To her and God up above;
I'll always be grateful for showing me their compassion, and their true unconditional and unfailing love.

Someday my future will again be as bright as the sun;
Until then I will carry with me cherished memories of her and of all our fun.

Once again this ole cowboy into the sunset must ride;
But this time in my life I won't be alone, as God will be riding with me, by my side.

As I ride off I will have a smile on my face;
Remembering her sweet ways and of her tender and warm embrace.

In my heart I will carry a song of our love from above;
And will always be thankful for her loving friendship and sweet, sweet love.

Vaya con Dios, mi Amor, will be the last words that I say;
As off into the sunset I will ride to face another challenge along,
"Life's Highway".

~~~

For I know the thoughts that I think toward you, saith the LORD, thoughts of peace, and not of evil, to give you an expected end.
Jeremiah 29:11

Philippians 4:13 I can do all things through Christ which strengthened me. Philippians 4:13

For with God nothing shall be impossible. Luke 1:37

And let us not grow weary of doing good, for in due season we will reap, if we do not give up. Galatians 6:9

And we know that all things work together for good to them that love God, to them who are the called according to his purpose.
Romans 8:28

He will wipe away every tear from their eyes, and death shall be no more, neither shall there be mourning, nor crying, nor pain anymore, for the former things have passed away."
Revelation 21:4

And so we know and rely on the love God has for us.
God is love. Whoever lives in love lives in God, and God in them. 1 John 4:16

Michael Gasaway

Blossom Forth

They come in many shapes, sizes and colors it seems;
Soft, delicate and fragrant, they can sweeten your dreams.

All start out the same, closed up waiting to blossom;
Then one day they unfold exposing their true beauty to some.

As time goes by their true inner beauty is exposed more each day;
Unfolding as their beauty blossoms as if in some magical ballet.

Some say a rose by any other name is still a rose actually;
But the true rose is a woman that has blossomed to fulfill her true destiny.

Her many layers take time to unfold and reveal;
The beauty that awaits those special few, it will seem so unreal.

Yes, you can learn a lot about women by studying this delicate flower;
You will see their real beauty, passion, inner strength and real power.

Both take time and the right conditions to blossom forth into the world;
What a magnificent sight to see, when they are complete and unfurled.

Enjoy their beauty, softness and the special fragrance that fills the air;
Always treat each with tender care and realize how special and rare.

For if you fail handle them with special loving care;
You'll feel their pain, making you very aware they were once there.

Give thanks to God if you have one in your life this day;
For when the time comes, you will see a magnificent display.

Thank God each day for the "roses" that grow and brighten our days;
Be patient, loving and listen carefully, and one day you just may hear one say……

~~~

You are altogether beautiful, my love; there is no flaw in you.
Song of Solomon 4:7

An excellent wife who can find? She is far more precious than jewels. Proverbs 31:10

Out of Zion, the perfection of beauty, God hath shined. Psalm 50:2

Behold, you are beautiful, my love, behold, you are beautiful!
Song of Solomon 4:1

Judge not according to the appearance, but judge righteous judgment. John 7:24

And your renown went forth among the nations because of your beauty, for it was perfect through the splendor that I had bestowed on you, declares the Lord God.
Ezekiel 16:14

Michael Gasaway

Loves Precious Flame

Loves precious flame once burned between them hotter than the sun;
Together over the years in love they had run.

Then without each other realizing, loves flame started to flicker;
The wave of love they had shared was becoming a mere ripple in the water.

No one seems to understand why or how the flame goes out;
There are times it just flickers away or goes with a shout.

Sometimes there is a choice that is made by one or the other;
Then the truth comes out as one does discover.

Love is all about doing what is right for the right reasons;
This should always be the case regardless of life's seasons.

Communication always seems to be an early causality when you look back;
By then it seems to be too late as love has gone way off the track.

Don't let Loves precious flame flicker and die in your life;
Hold on loosely to it and each other regardless of the strife.

Put each other first in everything that you do each day;
Always make time daily and come together and pray.

Love's precious flame will then burn all of your days here to be;
You will feel it still as you both walk together through eternity.

~~~

*Set me as a seal upon your heart, as a seal upon your arm, for love is strong as death, jealousy is fierce as the grave. Its flashes are flashes of fire, the very flame of the Lord. Many waters cannot quench love, neither can floods drown it. If a man offered for love all the wealth of his house, he would be utterly despised.
Song of Solomon 8:6-7*

*He that loveth not knoweth not God; for God is love.
1 John 4:8*

Let your speech be always with grace, seasoned with salt, that ye may know how ye ought to answer every man. Colossians 4:6

Therefore to him that knoweth to do good, and doeth it not, to him it is sin. James 4:17

Love bears all things, believes all things, hopes all things, endures all things. 1 Corinthians 13:7 ESV

So now faith, hope, and love abide, these three; but the greatest of these is love. 1 Corinthians 13:13

Lying lips are an abomination to the Lord, but those who act faithfully are his delight. Proverbs 12:22

Above all, keep loving one another earnestly, since love covers a multitude of sins. 1 Peter 4:8

Michael Gasaway

Time

Time it is slowly slipping by;
There are no more words to say or tears to cry.

He doesn't understand why things turn out the way they do;
There are times you're just left feeling empty and oh so blue.

You do your best and at life try to succeed;
It's hard to move on sometimes and really believe.

Not knowing what the future holds as he moves on;
Maybe God will answer his prayers with the dawn.

The deals he makes inside his head;
Does he play black or does he play red?

Is it to the right he turns or to the left?
What difference does it make when all has been said?

So lost he feels and so very much alone;
Now on he goes alone with a heart slowly turning to stone.

Thinking back he wonders why he had lived when others did die;
The river of tears have since dried up that he cried.

Some people say that if it's meant to be it will be;
So they just sit back and try to wait patiently.

God gave us all free will to make our choices in life;
Sometimes the choices made by another will cause the strife.

It was not God who led him down the trail this time;
The choice of another changed his path he thought, not mine.

But on he must go and see it through to the end;
In his heart he knows that God will bless and favor him once again.

Little did he know that God was already working on it from up above;
He was already preparing and leading him towards a perfect love.

Now he rides together with the angel of his dreams;
So never give up on love or God no matter how dark it seems.

∼∼∼

……. Weeping may tarry for the night, but joy comes with the morning. Psalm 30:5

For I know the thoughts that I think toward you, saith the L<small>ORD</small>, thoughts of peace, and not of evil, to give you an expected end. Jeremiah 29:11

I can do all things through Christ which strengtheneth me. Philippians 4:13

For with God nothing shall be impossible. Luke 1:37

And let us not grow weary of doing good, for in due season we will reap, if we do not give up. Galatians 6:9

For everything there is a season, and a time for every matter under heaven: Ecclesiastes 3:1

Michael Gasaway

Stories and Lies

She had not been careful of the stories and lies that she once did tell;
Someday they will return to haunt her and put her through a living hell.

It seemed so innocent to her at the time the words that she spoke;
Not realizing then that one day it would be her words that would make it hard to cope.

Sometimes people say things just to make themselves feel good inside;
But then those same words come back to tear them up 'til they feel like they want to die.

There are those that always believe it's just all about them;
Seems they are always the first to point their finger and condemn.

Some won't accept the truth that they were in fact part of the blame;
Their pride won't let them admit their own failures and why it went down in flames.

Words can cause more damage than any weapon known to man;
Cutting deeper and causing more pain, that is almost impossible to withstand.

So be careful of the words and lies that you may say each day;
They will be returned to you someday leaving you with nothing to say.

Always do and say what is right in the eyes of God above;
Just do and say that which is true and comes from your heart with love.

Go back before it's too late and make things right with the actions you have said and done;
Don't be so proud as to not ask for forgiveness and seek absolution.

~~~

If you are snared in the words of your mouth, caught in the words of your mouth, Proverbs 6:2

Let your speech always be gracious, seasoned with salt, so that you may know how you ought to answer each person. Colossians 4:6

Whoever keeps his mouth and his tongue keeps himself out of trouble. Proverbs 21:23

There is one whose rash words are like sword thrusts, but the tongue of the wise brings healing. Proverbs 12:18

Death and life are in the power of the tongue, and those who love it will eat its fruits. Proverbs 18:21

For by your words you will be justified, and by your words you will be condemned. Matthew 12:37

Let no corrupting talk come out of your mouths, but only such as is good for building up, as fits the occasion, that it may give grace to those who hear. Ephesians 4:29

I tell you, on the day of judgment people will give account for every careless word they speak, Matthew 12:36

Let the words of my mouth and the meditation of my heart be acceptable in your sight, O Lord, my rock and my redeemer. Psalm 19:14

Gracious words are like a honeycomb, sweetness to the soul and health to the body. Proverbs 16:24

Do you see a man who is hasty in his words? There is more hope for a fool than for him. Proverbs 29:20

Let no one deceive you with empty words, for because of these things the wrath of God comes upon the sons of disobedience. Ephesians 5:6

Michael Gasaway

Because of You

Because of you she thought, I had given so much;
But still she recalled the warmth of his touch.

She watched as the rain fell harder from the sky;
A flood of memories in her mind went rushing by.

In the distance she could hear the thunder roll;
The past several months had taken their emotional toll.

Her faith had been shaken by the events of the past year;
The music and sounds of the past she could still hear.

It was decision time she knew in her heart within;
Yes, time to move on and to begin again.

Don't let the past hold you back and cause you more pain;
Let the sad tears be washed away like a cleansing rain.

The past is where it all belonged and she vowed to put it all there to stay;
Letting go and moving on in search of brighter days.

Sometimes you have to just let go and move on in life;
Put the past behind you along with all of the strife.

Completely open up your heart to God up above;
Let Him guide and direct your steps with His perfect love.

Time has moved on now and so has she at last;
No longer is she haunted by painful memories from her past.

As on cue as if it had been planned all along to be;
A special cowboy entered her life so sweet and innocently.

You can't meet or achieve the desires of your heart;
If your still holding on to the past and refuse a fresh start.

Put the past behind you where it belongs without delay;
Your dream is awaiting you and may be just a day away.

∾∾∾

Thou tellest my wanderings: put thou my tears into thy bottle:
Psalm 56:8

Behold, I will do a new thing; now it shall spring forth; shall ye not know it? I will even make a way in the wilderness, and rivers in the desert. Isaiah 43:19

The heart of man plans his way, but the Lord establishes his steps.
Proverbs 16:9

I will instruct thee and teach thee in the way which thou shalt go: I will guide thee with mine eye. Psalm 32:8

For I know the plans I have for you, declares the Lord, plans for welfare and not for evil, to give you a future and a hope.
Jeremiah 29:11

He heals the brokenhearted and binds up their wounds.
Psalm 147:3

Michael Gasaway

You Never Know

The love they felt for one another some could not perceive;
It was a love so pure and true, an eternal love you see.

Some thought that he would cut and run and disappear with the setting sun;
Like so many others may have done.

She was fighting a daily battle for her very life;
But tall he stood by her side through all the adversity and strife.

Time and again he was right there with her to see;
Together he stood with her so never alone would she be.

A special kind of love was theirs, that people to this day still talk;
He was her man that not only did the talk, but would walk the walk.

They had a love for one another that was so sweet and pure;
It was the kind of love that everyone secretly longs for.

Their time together was all to brief, but yet so sweet and complete;
But what a love it showed to everyone, when together they would meet.

How she had always longed for a special unconditional kind of love;
She found that love in the end, heaven sent from up above.

Love had come to them in a different manner, that is so very true;
But you never know how real love will come seeking you.

So learn from their true story of a special kind of love God sent;
When you find that special one, make every loving moment well spent.

Dance together like no one is watching you;
One another do love with all your heart and to each other, always be true.

Kiss passionately and often every chance that you get;
You never know when it will be yours or theirs, last sunset.

Walk on the beach and making hearts in the sand;
Always be together and holding onto each other's hand.

Laugh and love together in everything that you do;
And never miss a chance to tell each other, "I Love You".

∼∼∼

Let all that you do be done in love. 1 Corinthians 16:14

And above all these put on love, which binds everything together in perfect harmony. Colossians 3:14

We love because he first loved us. 1 John 4:19

*Beloved, let us love one another, for love is from God, and whoever loves has been born of God and knows God.
1 John 4:7*

*"He will wipe away every tear from their eyes, and death shall be no more, neither shall there be mourning, nor crying, nor pain anymore, for the former things have passed away."
Revelation 21:4*

Love is patient and kind; love does not envy or boast; it is not arrogant or rude. It does not insist on its own way; it is not irritable or resentful; it does not rejoice at wrongdoing, but rejoices with the truth. Love bears all things, believes all things, hopes all things, endures all things. Love never ends. 1 Corinthians 13:4-8

Michael Gasaway

So Right

They rode down the trail guided along by glimmering beams of moonlight;
In her heart she gave thanks, and felt that this was oh so right.

Her heart had been wounded by loves deception in the not too distant past;
Now it seems that God had brought to her, a true love that will last.

Letting go of the past had not been an easy thing for her to achieve;
But she had read a poem one day and it had made her believe.

The poem had spoken of letting go of loves hold from yesterday;
Let go and let God's will be done, then let Him lead your way.

He will lead you and guide you into a bright future full of love;
It's not easy, so keep trusting and believing, and have faith in God up above.

Now together side by side, she and her new love ride down life's trail;
This is a love so strong and true, a real love that will never fail.

You can't move forward in life, until you decide to just let the past go;
Then God can direct your steps and the right path to you, He will show.

This new love in her life, she knew that she would never have found;
If with the past she hadn't just let go, that had kept her heart bound.

Do what you can to make things right with your yesterdays;
But in the end just trust in God above and always seek His ways.

Then hold your head high with a smile on your face;
Walk into tomorrow with a song in your heart of God's amazing grace.

∾∾∾

Delight yourself in the Lord, and he will give you the desires of your heart. Psalm 37:4

Commit your way to the Lord; trust in him, and he will act. Psalm 37:5

For where your treasure is, there your heart will be also. Matthew 6:21

The plans of the heart belong to man, but the answer of the tongue is from the Lord. All the ways of a man are pure in his own eyes, but the Lord weighs the spirit. Commit your work to the Lord, and your plans will be established. Proverbs 16:1-3

The heart of man plans his way, but the Lord establishes his steps. Proverbs 16:9

Michael Gasaway

Forever and a Day

This cowboy's life's journey had taken him both far and wide;
All along he had always felt a missing piece deep inside.

Then one night under that star filled Texas sky;
Into his life she came and flashed him that million dollar smile.

She seemed to appear out of a romantic dream somewhere;
The cowboy couldn't believe his eyes, her beauty was so rare.

It was just as he had dreamed those many years before;
How she'd walked right up, kissed him passionately, opening loves door.

He had read of her in another life and time someplace;
Her crystal blue eyes, her raven hair and her beautiful angelic face.

His heart began to beat faster at the sound of her sweet voice;
Of feeling her gentle touch and lips so soft, warm and moist.

They had connected with their hearts long before their lips ever met;
Closer they became each feeling a romantic rush, now part of a love duet.

With each passing day the nearer they became and deeper in love;
Each day he thanks God for sending this angel to him from above.

Now always on each other's mind and forever in each heart they will stay;
That is the way it was written for them long ago, forever and a day.

∼∼∼

Oh, give thanks to the Lord, for He is good! For His mercy endures forever. 1 Chronicles 16:34

Delight yourself in the Lord, and he will give you the desires of your heart. Psalm 37:4

Let all that you do be done in love. 1 Corinthians 16:14

And above all these put on love, which binds everything together in perfect harmony. Colossians 3:14

We love because he first loved us. 1 John 4:19

Beloved, let us love one another, for love is from God, and whoever loves has been born of God and knows God. 1 John 4:7

Love is patient and kind; love does not envy or boast; it is not arrogant or rude. It does not insist on its own way; it is not irritable or resentful; it does not rejoice at wrongdoing, but rejoices with the truth. Love bears all things, believes all things, hopes all things, endures all things. Love never ends. 1 Corinthians 13:4-8

Michael Gasaway

Complete

Oh how she does light up the stage;
She puts the crowd into a musical rage.

Her blue eyes how they sparkle and shine;
When she sings her voice is so divine.

The guitar riffs that flow from her strings;
Get the crowd on their feet and satisfy's their cravings.

Night after night such an electrifying performance she gives;
It's always the same, be it cowboys or executives.

Music is her life and singing fills her soul;
But there are times that the road does take its toll;

Sometimes you need a break and just get away;
So that in the end your music you don't betray.

She needs other things in her life now to feel complete;
A good man by her side would be so very sweet.

A special man that she could love and ride side by side;
Yes that special man to whom she could be his bride.

Such is a dream that fills her heart way down deep;
To marry her man and in his arms each night, fall asleep.

~~~

Sing unto him, sing psalms unto him: talk ye of all his wondrous works. Psalm 105:2

Speaking to yourselves in psalms and hymns and spiritual songs, singing and making melody in your heart to the Lord; Ephesians 5:19

I will sing unto the Lord as long as I live: I will sing praise to my God while I have my being. Psalm 104:33

Oh come, let us sing to the Lord; let us make a joyful noise to the rock of our salvation! Psalm 95:1

Praise him with the tambourine and dancing; praise him with strings and flutes! Psalm 150:4

Delight thyself also in the Lord: and he shall give thee the desires of thine heart. Psalm 37:4

Commit thy way unto the Lord; trust also in him; and he shall bring it to pass. Psalm 37:5

Michael Gasaway

Words

Words are but seeds that we plant and sometimes they grow;
Be careful of the words that you sow.

Yes words mean things I've been told;
And it doesn't matter if you're young or old.

The words you speak can be a blessing or cut like a knife;
Don't allow your words to cause any strife.

Your words can mend or break a heart in two;
Then sometimes they just come back to haunt you.

Children are the most susceptible to the words you use;
Speak words of wisdom and love, and never verbally abuse.

Choose carefully the words that you speak;
Speaking kind words does not mean that you're weak.

Use your words to build and do praise;
Help another see through their painful haze.

Speak words of truth when it is right;
Then speak words of love into the night.

They may not remember but they will never forget the words you spoke;
Let them remember that your words always gave them hope.

∾∾∾

Whoever keeps his mouth and his tongue keeps himself out of trouble. Proverbs 21:23

Death and life are in the power of the tongue, and those who love it will eat its fruits. Proverbs 18:21

For by your words you will be justified, and by your words you will be condemned. Matthew 12:37

Let no corrupting talk come out of your mouths, but only such as is good for building up, as fits the occasion, that it may give grace to those who hear. Ephesians 4:29

*I tell you, on the day of judgment people will give account for every careless word they speak,
Matthew 12:36*

*Let the words of my mouth and the meditation of my heart be acceptable in your sight, O Lord, my rock and my redeemer.
Psalm 19:14*

A time to tear, and a time to sew; a time to keep silence, and a time to speak Ecclesiastes 3:7

Gracious words are like a honeycomb, sweetness to the soul and health to the body. Proverbs 16:24

Do you see a man who is hasty in his words? There is more hope for a fool than for him. Proverbs 29:20

*Let no one deceive you with empty words, for because of these things the wrath of God comes upon the sons of disobedience.
Ephesians 5:6*

*The words of a wise man's mouth win him favor, but the lips of a fool consume him. The beginning of the words of his mouth is foolishness, and the end of his talk is evil madness. A fool multiplies words, though no man knows what is to be, and who can tell him what will be after him?
Ecclesiastes 10:12-14*

Michael Gasaway

She Cries Out

Crying out from the emotional pain that she felt deep inside;
She asks God to help her, but this time also asking Him to be her guide.

It has been a long journey for her down life's highway;
Filled with heart ache and loss had been so many of her days.

So many times she felt like giving in and just quit;
But when these times came upon her she would not submit.

In her heart and soul she knew that God for her had a perfect plan;
Each day she went on step by step through loves wasteland.

Too many times she had rushed ahead in search of love and happiness;
There she found herself off the right path that God had set forth by being too anxious.

Through life we all have been guilty and strayed the same each day;
We get in a hurry and try to rush doing things our own way.

Little do we seem to understand at the time as we pray to God above?
God will always answer our prayers in time with His perfect love.

Now into her life he came as part of God's perfect plan one day;
Yes, a smiling cowboy that God had sent to show her the right way.

You never know when or how God answers the prayers you have prayed;
Just stay faithful and never give up and His word trust and obey.

Now into the future she goes and it looks so very bright;
Side by side with her cowboy and a love that feels so right.

Never give up and always trust that God has a perfect plan for your life;
Then always trust and believe that he will deliver you from all strife.

Now faith is the substance of things hoped for, the evidence of things not seen. Hebrews 11:1

And we know that all things work together for good to them that love God, to them who are the called according to his purpose. Romans 8:28

"He will wipe away every tear from their eyes, and death shall be no more, neither shall there be mourning, nor crying, nor pain anymore, for the former things have passed away." Revelation 21:4

And let us not grow weary of doing good, for in due season we will reap, if we do not give up. Galatians 6:9

For with God nothing shall be impossible. Luke 1:37

For I know the thoughts that I think toward you, saith the L<small>ORD</small>, thoughts of peace, and not of evil, to give you an expected end. Jeremiah 29:11

*For still the vision awaits its appointed time; it hastens to the end— it will not lie. If it seems slow, wait for it; it will surely come; it will not delay.
Habakkuk 2:3*

But they who wait for the Lord shall renew their strength; they shall mount up with wings like eagles; they shall run and not be weary; they shall walk and not faint. Isaiah 40:31

Michael Gasaway

It's Time

It's time to reignite that fire within her soul;
To move forward and let God have complete control.

Time to move on from loves wasteland;
Let go of the past and really follow God's plan.

The future will be brighter when she lets God have His way;
God will always let you know when it's time to let go and breakaway.

Now let go of the past but remember the lessons well;
Then pass them on to another when it's your turn to tell.

It won't be easy but nothing worthwhile is ever that;
Just let God guide your steps and don't look back.

Your destiny is once again in your hands to behold;
So pray to God each day then follow His plan as you are told.

He will direct each step you are to take;
Always beside you he will walk and never forsake.

Now with a spring in her step and a smile on her face;
She boldly goes forward to win at life's race.

She rides into tomorrow with a new song to sing;
A song of love and hope that tomorrow will bring.

As clear as a picture she now sees it in her mind's eye;
Just her and that special cowboy as into the sunset together they will ride.

~~~

For I know the thoughts that I think toward you, saith the Lord, thoughts of peace, and not of evil, to give you an expected end. Jeremiah 29:11

*The Lord is not slow to fulfill his promise as some count slowness, but is patient toward you, not wishing that any should perish, but that all should reach repentance.
2 Peter 3:9*

*And without faith it is impossible to please God, because anyone who comes to him must believe that he exists and that he rewards those who earnestly seek him.
Hebrews 11:6*

"Remember not the former things, nor consider the things of old. Behold, I am doing a new thing; now it springs forth, do you not perceive it? I will make a way in the wilderness and rivers in the desert. Isaiah 43:18-19

Let him kiss me with the kisses of his mouth— for your love is more delightful than wine. Song of Songs 1:2

*Casting all your care upon him; for he careth for you.
1 Peter 5:7*

Trust in the Lord with all thine heart; and lean not unto thine own understanding. In all thy ways acknowledge him, and he shall direct thy paths. Proverbs 3:5-6

*The heart of man plans his way, but the Lord establishes his steps
Proverbs 16:9*

Michael Gasaway

The Reason

You are the reason that my heart beats so;
It began when you created me so long ago.

I did not know then;
But now I know that in your thoughts I have always been.

You've been with me down every road and dusty trail;
Picking me up when I did fail.

Every time I sought you when trouble did appear;
I could feel your warm presence saying, "don't fear, I'm here".

You have always been there in good times and bad;
Always been with me no matter if I'm happy or sad.

Seldom did I take the time or say thank you as I should;
Still you loved me just as your word said you would.

Loving me and seeing me through each day of my life;
You were always walking with me, in peace, trouble or strife.

Seldom did I praise you as you deserve;
Didn't always offer to help or to serve.

There are so many things wrong that I have done;
But you still love me and welcome me as a son.

The change in me has been slow and at times I could not see;
Now I clearly gaze upon my true destiny.

My eyes that were closed can now see the door open wide;
With you always I will walk side by side.

The story does not end here but has only begun;
For my fate I will follow with the rising sun.

Thank you God for showing me the way and always being with me;
This poem is but my awkward way of saying thank you and praise be to thee.

∼∼∼

But the hour is coming, and is now here, when the true worshipers will worship the Father in spirit and truth, for the Father is seeking such people to worship him. John 4:23

Let everything that hath breath praise the Lord. Praise ye the Lord. Psalm 150:6

The steps of a good man are ordered by the Lord: and he delighted in his way. Psalm 37:23

For I know the thoughts that I think toward you, saith the Lord, thoughts of peace, and not of evil, to give you an expected end. Jeremiah 29:11

Whether you turn to the right or to the left, your ears will hear a voice behind you, saying, "This is the way; walk in it." Isaiah 30:21

Thy word is a lamp unto my feet, and a light unto my path. Psalm 119:105

I will instruct thee and teach thee in the way which thou shall go: I will guide thee with mine eye. Psalm 32:8

Michael Gasaway

The Cowboy

A cowboy was he from the very start;
From the boots to the Stetson, he truly looked the part.

The walk was there and so was the talk it seems;
Someday he would be the answer to a cowgirls dream.

Most of his friends were the horses he rode;
But a few people did measure up I'm told.

Tall in the saddle he would ride the trail;
This cowboy would never be the one to fail.

He loved the open spaces with a blanket of stars up above;
Life as a cowboy is what he would always love.

Hard and tough or gentle and kind he could be;
And there he would always be if a friend was ever in need.

His word was his bond and when he gave it they all knew;
This cowboy would always come through.

There were many stories about from where this cowboy came;
Most just said he wondered in with a heart gone lame.

Then as suddenly as he arrived off into the sunset he did ride away;
"God bless y'all and Happy Trails and maybe I'll see you along the trail one day" were the last words they heard him say.

~~~

But the God of all grace, who hath called us unto his eternal glory by Christ Jesus, after that ye have suffered a while, make you perfect, establish, strengthen, settle you.
1 Peter 5:10

And we know that all things work together for good to them that love God, to them who are the called according to his purpose.
Romans 8:28

Count it all joy, my brothers, when you meet trials of various kinds, James 1:2

I can do all things through him who strengthens me.
Philippians 4:13

And let us not grow weary of doing good, for in due season we will reap, if we do not give up. Galatians 6:9

For with God nothing shall be impossible. Luke 1:37

For I know the thoughts that I think toward you, saith the Lord, thoughts of peace, and not of evil, to give you an expected end.
Jeremiah 29:11

Michael Gasaway

Perceive, Believe and Receive

She didn't understand why her life was such a mess;
Couldn't understand why she was always under such stress.

In some areas her faith was strong as could be;
But in other areas of her life, her happiness she could not see.

Some days she prayed to God and did question, why;
On she went each day and did continue to try.

Try as you might in life, it's not always enough for you to find;
The beginning of the answers lies deep within your mind.

It came to her one spring day clear as could be;
Her perception of her life, in fact had become her reality.

You have to really perceive that which you pray for each day;
Then really believe and receive God's favor to come your way.

God answers your prayers in His own time as your faith perceives;
Never Give Up on your dreams and keep seeking them until you receive.

He will answer your prayers and give you the desires of your heart;
You must see it, believe it and receive it in order to do your part.

Always be thankful for what you have and that which is to come;
Your happiness and dreams are like a budding flower that in time you know will fully blossom.

~~~

Therefore I tell you, whatever you ask in prayer, believe that you have received it, and it will be yours. Mark 11:24

*Be delighted with the Lord.
Then He will give you all the desires of your heart. Psalms 37:4*

And Jesus said to him, "if you can'! All things are possible for one who believes." Mark 9:23

"And whatever you ask in prayer, you will receive, if you have faith." Matthew 21:22

I can do all things through Christ which strengthened me. Philippians 4:13

And let us not grow weary of doing good, for in due season we will reap, if we do not give up. Galatians 6:9

*"For it is commendable if someone bears up under the pain of unjust suffering because they are conscious of God." 1 Peter 2:19
But you, take courage! Do not let your hands be weak, for your work shall be rewarded." 2 Chronicles 15:7*

And we know that all things work together for good to them that love God, to them who are the called according to his purpose. Romans 8:28

Rejoice always, pray without ceasing, give thanks in all circumstances; for this is the will of God in Christ Jesus for you. 1 Thessalonians 5:16-18

For with God nothing shall be impossible. Luke 1:37

For I know the thoughts that I think toward you, saith the LORD, thoughts of peace, and not of evil, to give you an expected end. Jeremiah 29:11

Michael Gasaway

You Will Achieve

A crystal blue sky was giving way to dark clouds of gray;
In her heart she felt the same as her feelings for him began to fade.

Broken promises, lies and a love that became untrue;
Thinking back, how could this all happen and now, what was she to do.

It's not easy to keep believing, when your life comes apart at the seams;
In an instant, gone it seems are all of your hopes and dreams.

Why she thought does it have to end, especially in this way;
How does one reach the point and just throw a love and life away?

She had won and lost at love in life many times before;
But never so lost has she felt as with the closing of this door.

Time to begin anew she felt within her broken heart;
Now was time for her to move on and find a brand new start.

Remembering back to a book she had read once upon a time;
The book read of never giving up and of finding true love, written in rhyme.

Speaking to her heart of how to move on and let go of your past life;
How to cowgirl up and pray to God for peace during this time of strife.

Now time has moved on, slowly it seems, and so has she;
It wasn't easy dealing with her heart ache and learning how a bright future to see.

Her future is now brighter than she ever imagined it could be;
Learning how to forgive, move on in life and really how to believe.

You, like her have the power within if you just believe and perceive;
Trust in God above and let Him lead, guide and direct you and one day your dreams, you will achieve.

The Lord is near to all who call on him, to all who call on him in truth. Psalm 145:18

Delight thyself also in the LORD: and he shall give thee the desires of thine heart. Commit thy way unto the LORD; trust also in him; and he shall bring it to pass. Psalm 37:4-5

The steadfast love of the Lord never ceases; his mercies never come to an end; they are new every morning; great is your faithfulness. Lamentations 3:22-23

Trust in the Lord with all your heart, and do not lean on your own understanding. In all your ways acknowledge him, and he will make straight your paths. Proverbs 3:5-6

Cast all your anxiety on him because he cares for you. 1 Peter 5:7

And let us not grow weary of doing good, for in due season we will reap, if we do not give up. Galatians 6:9

Now faith is the substance of things hoped for, the evidence of things not seen.
Hebrews 11:1

Michael Gasaway

One Day

Her dark hair glistened like that of an eagle's wing;
She had eyes that were as blue as the bluebonnets in the Texas spring.

Smiling and laughing she could disarm you with ease;
Such a sweet demeanor she has, and with a tantalizing southern accent to please.

Struggles and hardships she has seen in her life;
The desire of her heart was to be someone's loving and devoted wife.

To be loved by a special man that she knew one day would arrive;
In her heart she knew that he was the one to again make her really feel alive.

It was so clear for her to see in her mind's eye;
He would be a special man who would love her and always be by her side.

Then one day it happened in of all places a Wal-Mart aisle;
She ran into this handsome cowboy that tipped his hat and made her smile.

Neither was really looking when God brought them together on that fateful day;
Just goes to show you that God and love will always find a way.

So never give up on love or God in heaven above;
One day He will send you that special person for you to always love.

Now into the sunset together they ride, hand n' hand;
That beautiful sweet southern belle and that handsome Texas man.

~~~

And let us not grow weary of doing good, for in due season we will reap, if we do not give up. Galatians 6:9

For with God nothing shall be impossible. Luke 1:37

For I know the thoughts that I think toward you, saith the LORD, thoughts of peace, and not of evil, to give you an expected end. Jeremiah 29:11

And we know that all things work together for good to them that love God, to them who are the called according to his purpose. Romans 8:28

Rejoice evermore. Pray without ceasing. In everything give thanks: for this is the will of God in Christ Jesus concerning you. 1 Thessalonians 5:16-18

"But you, take courage! Do not let your hands be weak, for your work shall be rewarded." 2 Chronicles 15:7

And the LORD God said, It is not good that the man should be alone; I will make him an help meet for him. Genesis 2:18

Take delight in the LORD, and he will give you the desires of your heart. Psalm 37:4

Michael Gasaway

Reflections

Watching the sun slowly fall across the distant tree line;
Another year was gone with the ever marching of time.

A time for reflection and thinking about her past;
She remembered back to that special man and a love that didn't last.

The amber colors and pink clouds danced above the setting sun;
Soon it would be time and another year would be done.

It had been for her a year of hard choices and some regrets;
Some she questioned and some she just tried to forget.

Wondering if the choices she had made, had really been right;
Why then was she crying tears late into the night?

Sometimes we follow only our heads instead of our hearts;
That's when the choices we make can really tear us apart.

Always let your heart be your guide from God up above;
Let the choices you make, always be made with love.

If you can't go back and change what you have done;
Then maybe it's time to start fresh again with the rising of the sun.

Awaken tomorrow with a new purpose and a new life to begin;
Time to Cowgirl Up; seek out your dreams and your destiny to win.

~~~

All Scripture is breathed out by God and profitable for teaching, for reproof, for correction, and for training in righteousness,
2 Timothy 3:16

How much better [is it] to get wisdom than gold! And to get understanding rather to be chosen than silver!
Proverbs 16:16

[There is] treasure to be desired and oil in the dwelling of the wise; but a foolish man spendeth it up.
Proverbs 21:20

For I know the thoughts that I think toward you, saith the LORD, thoughts of peace, and not of evil, to give you an expected end.
Jeremiah 29:11

For this is our God forever and ever: he will be our guide even unto death. Psalms 48:14

For now we see only a reflection as in a mirror; then we shall see face to face. Now I know in part; then I shall know fully, even as I am fully known.
1 Corinthians 13:12

For still the vision awaits its appointed time; it hastens to the end— it will not lie. If it seems slow, wait for it; it will surely come; it will not delay. Habakkuk 2:3

Michael Gasaway

The Cowboy Rides Away

It was fun while it lasted and oh the good times that they had;
Alone now he will ride away just feeling lonely and very sad.

Into the sunset he will ride alone with a heart gone lame;
Sometimes he does wonder inside if he'll ever be the same.

Not sure at all of what tomorrow may bring;
But for now he thinks he'll give up chasing that gold ring.

Not sure at all where this trail will lead him that he takes;
He just knows that God rides with him and that He'll never forsake.

At times he does wonder what God has in store for him;
Because all he feels now is very lonely and empty within.

Deep inside, he knows that his future will be bright once again;
As for now he doesn't know where and when this trail may end.

Now it's time for him to saddle up and for the Cowboy to ride away;
He just says; "God bless y'all and Happy Trails and maybe I'll see you along the trail one day".

His story doesn't end here but is just the beginning it seems;
For way down the trail and in a new town he rode into his dreams.

An angel with raven hair and sapphire blue eyes smiled his way;
They spoke only with their eyes and touched with their hearts on that fall Texas day.

Now into the future together they go riding side by side;
His end was only the beginning of a new life that God sent down from heaven on high.

So never give up or think that this is your end of life or love;
You never know when God will bless you with a new life and love from above.

~~~

In all thy ways acknowledge him, and he shall direct thy paths.
Proverbs 3:6

The Lord is not slow in keeping his promise, as some understand slowness. Instead he is patient with you, not wanting anyone to perish, but everyone to come to repentance. 2 Peter 3:9

And let us not grow weary of doing good, for in due season we will reap, if we do not give up. Galatians 6:9

Love is patient and kind. Love is not jealous or boastful or proud or rude. It does not demand its own way. It is not irritable, and it keeps no record of being wronged. It does not rejoice about injustice but rejoices whenever the truth wins out. Love never gives up, never loses faith, is always hopeful, and endures through every circumstance. Prophecy and speaking in unknown languages and special knowledge will become useless. But love will last forever!
1 Corinthians 13:4-8

Delight yourself in the Lord, and he will give you the desires of your heart. Psalm 37:4

He heals the brokenhearted and binds up their wounds.
Psalm 147:3